KNOWING MY INNER SELF

APPLIED SPIRITUALITY FOR TEENAGERS

Fazel Naghdy

Copyright © 2014 Fazel Naghdy
All rights reserved.

ISBN: 978-0-909991-06-7

DEDICATION

To Golshah, my children and grandchildren

CONTENTS

DEDICATION III
CONTENTS V
ACKNOWLEDGMENTS XIII
PREFACE 1
SECTION I – THE EMERGENCE OF HUMAN BEINGS 5

1 EMERGENCE OF THE UNIVERSE 7
   1.1 INTRODUCTION 7
   1.2 BIBLE STORY OF CREATION 8
   1.3 BIG-BANG THEORY 9
   1.4 ACTIVITIES 11
      1.4.1 Multiple choice questions 11
      1.4.2 Short-answer questions 13
      1.4.3 Projects 14

2 EVOLUTION OF THE UNIVERSE 15
   2.1 INTRODUCTION 15
   2.2 ORDINARY MATTER 16
      2.2.1 Atomic structure of matter 16
      2.2.2 Different phases of matter 16
   2.3 EVOLUTION OF MATTER IN THE UNIVERSE 17
   2.4 WHO IS 'ABDU'L-BAHÁ? 18
   2.5 ACTIVITIES 19
      2.5.1 Multiple choice questions 19
      2.5.2 Short-answer questions 21
      2.5.3 Projects 22

3 EMERGENCE OF LIFE 23

3.1	INTRODUCTION	23
3.2	LIFE	24
3.3	ORIGIN AND SOURCE OF LIFE	24
3.4	LIFE IN THE UNIVERSE	25
3.5	WHO IS BAHÁ'U'LLÁH?	26
3.6	ACTIVITIES	27
3.6.1	*Multiple choice questions*	*27*
3.6.2	*Short-answer questions*	*29*
3.6.3	*Projects*	*30*

4 DIVERSITY OF LIFE ON EARTH 31

4.1	INTRODUCTION	31
4.2	HIERARCHY OF LIFE	32
4.3	CATEGORIES OF EXISTENCE	33
4.3.1	*Mineral Kingdom*	*33*
4.3.2	*Vegetable Kingdom*	*33*
4.3.3	*Animal Kingdom*	*34*
4.3.4	*Human Kingdom*	*34*
4.4	ANIMATING POWER IN EACH KINGDOM	34
4.5	ACTIVITIES	36
4.5.1	*Multiple choice questions*	*36*
4.5.2	*Short-answer questions*	*38*
4.5.3	*Projects*	*40*

5 EVOLUTION OF LIFE ON EARTH 41

5.1	INTRODUCTION	41
5.2	CONCEPT OF EVOLUTION	42
5.2.1	*Common descent*	*42*
5.2.2	*Mechanisms of evolution*	*43*
5.3	EVOLUTION AND MAN	44
5.4	ACTIVITIES	46
5.4.1	*Multiple choice questions*	*46*
5.4.2	*Short-answer questions*	*48*
5.4.3	*Projects*	*49*

SECTION II – THE NATURE OF HUMAN BEINGS 51

6 REALITY OF MAN 53

6.1	INTRODUCTION	53
6.2	COMPLEXITY OF HUMAN REALITY	54
6.3	A LOGICAL MODEL FOR HUMAN REALITY	55
6.4	ACTIVITIES	57

    6.4.1   Multiple choice questions.. 57
    6.4.2   Short-answer questions 59
    6.4.3   Projects 61

7 HUMAN PHYSICAL REALITY... 62
  7.1   INTRODUCTION 62
  7.2   HUMAN BODY 63
  7.3   SENSORY PERCEPTION 63
  7.4   INSTINCTIVE RESPONSES 64
  7.5   GENES AND INSTINCTS 66
  7.6   ACTIVITIES.. 68
    7.6.1   Multiple choice questions.. 68
    7.6.2   Short answer questions 70
    7.6.3   Projects 71

8 HUMAN INTELLECTUAL REALITY 73
  8.1   INTRODUCTION 73
  8.2   NATURE OF INTELLECTUAL REALITY 74
  8.3   INTELLECTUAL REALITY AND THE MIND 74
  8.4   OPERATION OF INTELLECTUAL REALITY 75
    8.4.1   Nature and function of the mind 76
  8.5   ACTIVITIES.. 78
    8.5.1   Multiple choice questions.. 78
    8.5.2   Short answer questions 80
    8.5.3   Projects 82

9 HUMAN SPIRITUAL REALITY.. 84
  9.1   INTRODUCTION 84
  9.2   EVIDENCES OF SPIRITUAL REALITY 85
  9.3   SPIRITUAL REALITY AND THE SOUL... 85
  9.4   POWERS AND FUNCTIONS OF THE SOUL.. 86
    9.4.1   Interaction with the physical world 87
    9.4.2   Identity of an individual 87
    9.4.3   Capacity for growth and transformation 87
    9.4.4   Spiritual perception 87
    9.4.5   Reflecting virtuous choices.. 88
    9.4.6   Assisting mental processes of the mind 88
  9.5   ACTIVITIES.. 90
    9.5.1   Multiple choice questions.. 90
    9.5.2   Short answer questions 92
    9.5.3   Projects 94

10 SELF 95
- 10.1 INTRODUCTION 95
- 10.2 IN SEARCH OF THE SELF 96
- 10.3 SELF IN RELIGION AND PHILOSOPHY 97
- 10.4 MODELLING SELF, BASED ON HUMAN REALITY 98
- 10.5 ACTIVITIES 100
  - 10.5.1 Multiple choice questions 100
  - 10.5.2 Short answer questions 102
  - 10.5.3 Projects 104

11 EGO 105
- 11.1 INTRODUCTION 105
- 11.2 DEFINITION OF THE EGO 106
- 11.3 INFLUENCE OF THE PHYSICAL-SELF ON THE EGO 106
- 11.4 INFLUENCE OF THE SPIRITUAL-SELF ON THE EGO 108
- 11.5 JOURNEY OF THE EGO 108
- 11.6 ACTIVITIES 110
  - 11.6.1 Double choice questions 110
  - 11.6.2 Short answer questions 111
- 11.7 PROJECT 113

12 INNER GIFTS AND CAPACITIES 114
- 12.1 INTRODUCTION 114
- 12.2 CAPACITIES WITHIN 114
- 12.3 PHYSICAL CAPACITIES 115
- 12.4 INTELLECTUAL CAPACITIES 116
- 12.5 SPIRITUAL CAPACITIES 117
- 12.6 CULTIVATING INNER CAPACITIES 117
- 12.7 ACTIVITIES 120
  - 12.7.1 Double choice questions 120
  - 12.7.2 Short answer questions 121
  - 12.7.3 Projects 124

13 FREE WILL AND MORAL CHOICES 126
- 13.1 INTRODUCTION 126
- 13.2 HUMAN FREE WILL 127
- 13.3 MAKING MORAL CHOICES 127
- 13.4 MORAL MOTIVATIONS 128
- 13.5 MORAL DEVELOPMENT 129
- 13.6 HEINZ DILEMMA 130
- 13.7 ACTIVITIES 133
  - 13.7.1 Double choice questions 133

      13.7.2 Short answer questions *134*
      13.7.3 Project *137*
  13.8 APPENDIX A - SELECTED LIST OF VIRTUES 138

14 SELF-RESPECT 141
  14.1 INTRODUCTION 141
  14.2 SELF-RESPECT 142
  14.3 RESPECTING THE PHYSICAL-SELF 143
  14.4 RESPECTING THE INTELLECTUAL-SELF 144
  14.5 RESPECTING THE SPIRITUAL-SELF 145
  14.6 ACTIVITIES 147
      14.6.1 Double choice questions *147*
      14.6.2 Reflecting on the "self" *147*
      14.6.3 Short answer questions *149*
      14.6.4 Assessing your "self" *150*
      14.6.5 Project *152*

SECTION III – CULTIVATING INNER CAPACITIES 153

15 PURPOSE OF HUMAN LIFE 155
  15.1 INTRODUCTION 155
  15.2 PURPOSEFULNESS OF THE UNIVERSE 156
  15.3 MATERIALISTIC PERSPECTIVE 156
  15.4 SPIRITUAL PERSPECTIVE 158
      15.4.1 Contributing to spiritual development *158*
      15.4.2 Contributing to an ever-advancing civilization *159*
  15.5 ACTIVITIES 160
      15.5.1 Double choice questions *160*
      15.5.2 Short answer questions *161*
      15.5.3 Project *164*

16 KNOWLEDGE, VOLITION, ACTION 165
  16.1 INTRODUCTION 165
  16.2 A STRATEGY FOR PERSONAL EFFORT 165
  16.3 CULTIVATING PHYSICAL CAPACITIES 167
  16.4 CULTIVATING INTELLECTUAL CAPACITIES 168
  16.5 CULTIVATING SPIRITUAL CAPACITIES 168
  16.6 ACTIVITIES 171
      16.6.1 Double choice questions *171*
      16.6.2 Short answer questions *172*
      16.6.3 Project *175*

17 EDUCATION 176

17.1	Introduction	176
17.2	Education and inner capacities	177
17.2.1	Physical education	178
17.2.2	Intellectual education	179
17.2.3	Spiritual education	180
17.3	Primary purpose of education	180
17.4	Activities	182
17.4.1	Double choice questions	182
17.4.2	Short answer questions	183
17.4.3	Project	186

18 RELIGION 187

18.1	Introduction	187
18.2	Definition of religion	188
18.3	Materialistic view on the nature of religion	189
18.4	Spiritual view on the nature of religion	190
18.5	True Educators	191
18.6	Activities	193
18.6.1	Double choice questions	193
18.6.2	Short answer questions	194
18.6.3	Project	197

19 FOUR SEASONS OF A RELIGION 199

19.1	Introduction	199
19.2	Physical world a counterpart of spiritual world	200
19.3	Spiritual cycle of religion	200
19.3.1	Spiritual springtime	201
19.3.2	Summer of achievement	201
19.3.3	Turbulent autumn	202
19.3.4	Winter of despondency	202
19.4	Concept of progressive revelation	203
19.5	Activities	205
19.5.1	Double choice questions	205
19.5.2	Short answer questions	206
19.5.3	Project	210

SECTION IV – A MYSTICAL JOURNEY 213

20 GOD, THE CREATOR 215

20.1	Introduction	215
20.2	Logical search for Creator	216
20.3	Historical roots of belief in God	217

- 20.4 NATURE OF GOD 218
- 20.5 KNOWLEDGE OF GOD 219
- 20.6 ACTIVITIES 221
  - 20.6.1 Double choice questions.. 221
  - 20.6.2 Short answer questions 222
  - 20.6.3 Project... 225

21 SPIRITUALITY 226
- 21.1 INTRODUCTION 226
- 21.2 MEANING OF SPIRITUALITY 227
- 21.3 SPIRITUALITY AND SCIENCE 228
- 21.4 SPIRITUALITY AND RELIGION 229
- 21.5 ACTIVITIES 231
  - 21.5.1 Double choice questions.. 231
  - 21.5.2 Short answer questions 232
  - 21.5.3 Project... 235

22 MYSTICAL SPIRITUALITY 237
- 22.1 INTRODUCTION 237
- 22.2 JOURNEY OF THE SOUL 238
- 22.3 DYNAMIC OF MYSTICAL SPIRITUALITY 239
  - 22.3.1 Knowledge: Knowledge of God............................. 240
  - 22.3.2 Volition: Love of God 241
  - 22.3.3 Action: Obedience and service............................. 242
- 22.4 ACTIVITIES 245
  - 22.4.1 Multiple Choice Questions 245
  - 22.4.2 Short answer questions 247
  - 22.4.3 Project... 250

23 TRUE HAPPINESS 251
- 23.1 INTRODUCTION 251
- 23.2 HAPPINESS 252
- 23.3 TRANSIENT HAPPINESS 253
- 23.4 TRUE HAPPINESS 254
- 23.5 INNER PEACE 256
- 23.6 ACTIVITIES 258
  - 23.6.1 Double choice questions.. 258
  - 23.6.2 Short answer questions 258
  - 23.6.3 Projects... 260

24 BUILDING AN EVER ADVANCING CIVILIZATION 261
- 24.1 INTRODUCTION 261

24.2	Human civilization	262
24.3	Human civilization and religion	263
24.4	Engaging in a spiritual enterprise	264
24.4.1	Spiritual education of children	265
24.4.2	Spiritual education of junior youth	266
24.5	Activities	268
24.5.1	Double choice questions	268
24.5.2	Short answer questions	269
24.5.3	Project	271

APPENDIX-FURTHER RESOURCES **273**
   Inspiring examples 273
   Guides on health and nutrition 273
   Resources on spiritual journey 274

INDEX **275**

ACKNOWLEDGMENTS

I would like to acknowledge the contribution of the many youths, participating in different courses of Education for Peace program in Australia over a period of nearly twenty years, that assisted me to develop and share the concepts presented in this book with other teenagers. I also wish to express my deep appreciation to Michael Thomas and Yvonne Woźniak who proofread and edited the book.

PREFACE

Knowing my inner self is written for teenagers to assist them in their journey to discover inner self and to cultivate their hidden capacities as they blossom from childhood to maturity. It explores answers to the fundamental questions that often occupy the mind of adolescents at some stage of their growth: What am I? Who am I? What is the purpose of my life? The concepts and issues associated with these questions are examined, and their implications for teenagers are highlighted.

The content of the book is inspired by universal spiritual principles, particularly the concepts taught by Bahá'u'lláh, the Prophet Founder of the Bahá'í Faith. The approach and pedagogy is the result of nearly twenty years of sharing these concepts with teenagers of different age groups in the Education for Peace Program offered by the Yerrinbool Bahá'í Centre of Learning in Australia.

The style of writing is simple but logical, and conclusions are reached through observation and reasoning. It simulates, as much as possible, a tutor-tutored relationship in which the tutor facilitates learning for an individual or a small group.

In summary, the book represents a manual on practical spirituality for teenagers and a workbook of activities to assist the reader to assimilate the concepts and apply them to personal situations. The concepts covered in the book and the material provided are generally useful for teenagers aged 15 years or over.

The book consists of four major parts:
a) The emergence of human beings
b) The nature of human beings
c) Cultivating inner capacities
d) A mystical journey

The focus of the first part of the book is on the evolution of life on the earth. An effort is made in this section to distinguish between the facts and theories surrounding the concept of evolution. It is now scientifically proven that the diverse organisms currently living on the earth have changed and been transformed over a long period of time. However, an analysis undertaken in this book, of different views including both materialist and spiritual, suggests that human beings have undergone a separate evolution to that of animals. Man has always been a distinct, original species, uniquely different from other animals, although sharing aspects of their physical appearance in the earlier stages of prehistory.

In part two the nature of man is studied. Through observation and reasoning it is demonstrated that a pure materialistic view is far from adequate to explain all the characteristics of man. A more complete model should embrace the physical, intellectual and spiritual aspects of man. Hence, the theme developed in the rest of the book is based on the assumption that man has three inter-related realities: the physical reality, the intellectual reality and the spiritual reality. Every human being is born with capacities embedded in each reality that should be cultivated and unfolded during the physical life.

In part three the purpose of man's physical life is examined. The cultivation of inner capacities, identified as a major objective of human life, is emphasised and practical steps to accomplish this are explored. The role of education and religion in the process of capacity building is highlighted.

The final part of the book looks into the mystical aspects of spiritual growth, which is the process of drawing closer to God through knowledge and recognition of His Manifestation, growing love of Him, and serving His Cause. Engaging in the spiritual education of children and junior youth is identified as an important service in this day and age, and a significant contribution towards building a materially and spiritually prosperous human civilization.

The book consists of 24 chapters. Each chapter starts with an introduction that highlights the key concepts addressed. The topic covered in the chapter is then explored in sections of relatively short length. The chapter then ends with a series of activities aimed at assisting the reader to assimilate the concepts. The activities are designed to stimulate thought and reflection at three levels: acquisition of the knowledge provided in each chapter, analysis of this knowledge and the application of this knowledge particularly to personal situations.

To derive the most benefit from your study, please follow the procedure explained below:

1. Read each chapter once to get an overview of the content.
2. Reread the chapter, but this time reflect on each paragraph to ensure that you fully grasp its meaning.
3. Complete the activities given for each chapter.
4. On the completion of a chapter, if there are still issues that you do not fully grasp, raise them with your friends and discuss them. This will give you a new insight and understanding on those issues that can significantly help you.

Fazel Naghdy

Section I – The emergence of human beings

1 Emergence of the Universe

1.1 Introduction

The origin, creation and evolution of the physical world have always been issues of interest and sometimes of concern to people. In the process of forming our identity, we need to develop a convincing explanation about who we are and how we relate to the world around us. Over the last six thousand years of human written history, many Prophets, philosophers and scientists have provided us with their views on the origin of the universe and the nature of man. In prehistoric times, before humans were able to write and read, their worldview was passed down to later generations through their oral traditions and through their paintings on the walls of the caves where they lived.

In this chapter, we will briefly explore how the universe consisting of stars and galaxies came into existence. We reflect on the Bible story of creation as well as the Big Bang theory that reflects one of the modern views supported by scientific and astronomical observations.

You need to reflect on and understand the following key points:

a) The Bible story of creation primarily describes how the earth and its creatures came into existence.
b) The Bible story is symbolic and cannot be accepted literally.
c) The Big Bang theory explains how the galaxies and stars were born as matter was compressed in a black hole.
d) The scientific evidence shows that the process of the birth and death of galaxies and stars is a continuous and self-perpetuating process.

e) The Big Bang theory does not explain where the original matter, the black hole, or the order governing the process of the birth and death of stars originated.

1.2 Bible story of creation

The universe consists of all physical entities of stars, planets and moons; space and time; all forms of matter and energy; as well as the physical laws that govern them. Humanity has always been curious to know how the universe was created. In the early stages of civilization when science and astronomy had not yet progressed, religion had the major role in explaining the process of creation. Perhaps the most dominant religious view on creation is the story described initially in the Bible and later, with some variations, in the Qur'án.

The Bible begins with the statement, *"In the beginning God created the heavens and the earth."*[1] The earth initially had no form, and was empty and dark. The Spirit of God moved over *"the face of the waters"* preparing to implement God's creative Word. God then began to speak into existence all of His creation. The Bible describes the day-by-day account of what happened as follows:

- **Day 1**–God created light and separated the light from the darkness, calling light "day" and darkness "night".
- **Day 2**–God created an expanse to separate the waters and called it "sky".
- **Day 3**–God created dry ground and gathered the waters, calling the dry ground "land" and the gathered waters "seas". On day three, God also created vegetation (the plants and trees).
- **Day 4**–God created the sun, the moon and the stars to give light to the earth, and to govern and separate the day from the night. Such creation also symbolically marks the seasons, the days and the years.
- **Day 5**–God created every living creature of the seas and every winged bird, blessing them to multiply and fill the waters and the sky with life.
- **Day 6**– God created Adam (man) and Eve (woman) in His own image to commune with Him. He blessed them and gave them every creature and the whole earth to rule over, to care for and to cultivate.

---

[1] Genesis, Chapter 1.

- **Day 7**–God rested on the seventh day after finishing His creation. He blessed this day and made it holy.

There are different interpretations of the creation story of the Bible. According to one of them, the Bible story of creation is primarily an explanation of how the earth and what is seen from the earth—including the sun, moon and the stars—came into existence. It does not provide any perspective on the creation of galaxies and the universe.

1.3 Big-Bang theory

Human intelligence cannot accept, affirm or imagine the processes involved in the story of creation as described in the Bible. Scientific and astronomical discoveries over the last two centuries portray a different picture of how the universe came into existence that is not compatible with the story described in the Bible. Hence, it is logical to consider that the Biblical story symbolically describes the spiritual events that occurred as a result of the forces released through the revelation of Moses.

Scientific discoveries indicate that the universe, consisting of galaxies, planets and stars, may have come into being through a tremendous explosion in one instant of time around fifteen billion years ago. This is known as the Big Bang Theory, and is an effort to explain what happened during and after that moment.

Scientists have been developing a better understanding of the Big Bang Theory as more discoveries are made. According to one version of the theory, the process occurred at the core of a "black hole" where there was intense gravitational pressure. In a "black hole" the pressure is so high that finite matter is squished into infinite density. The theory suggests that our universe came into existence when the finite matter acquired infinite density and became an infinitesimally small and infinitely hot point known as a singularity. After its initial appearance, this singularity underwent a sudden inflation, the Big Bang. Initially it expanded rapidly, then more gradually, as it cooled and evolved into the current universe. The evolution of the universe is apparently still continuing.

The theory does not explain where the initial matter or the black hole came from, or how the gravitational forces resulting in the Big Bang emerged. It also does not identify the source of law and order that have governed this process. It has only been concerned with the process by which our universe came into existence.

Observations made by astronomers indicate that the birth of new stars and galaxies is continually recurring through a self-perpetuating and cyclic process. New stars are created when a dying star, or supernova, explodes and shoots shock waves through clouds of cosmic gas and dust. The gas and dust are subsequently compressed, gravity kicks in, and new stars are born. Eventually, some of the stars will die in a fiery blast, triggering another cycle of birth and death. This recycling of stellar dust and gas occurs across the universe. The earth's own sun has descended from multiple generations of stars.

The question is whether there has really been only one Big Bang to start off the universe or whether our universe, like the stars and galaxies it encompasses, is also in a continual process of birth and death, or inflation and deflation, in what is known as the "Big Bounce". Cosmologists are also suggesting that there may be many universes in various stages of development, and there are several different theories about the way these "multiverses" interact. In any case, it would appear that the cycle of birth and death that we observe in the natural world on the earth also exists on a cosmological scale, and is part of the order built into the creation process. However, when individual physical entities are destroyed, their constituent elements continue to exist and recombine to form new physical entities. Thus, it can be said that though individual stars and galaxies have a beginning and an end, the physical world is infinite and eternal, having no beginning and no end.

1.4 Activities

1.4.1 Multiple choice questions

1. The creation story of the Bible is primary about the birth of _____.
    A. the earth and objects seen from the earth
    B. planets
    C. galaxies
    D. All of the above

2. According to the Bible, initially the earth _____.
    A. had no form
    B. was dark
    C. was empty
    D. All of the above

3. The Bible story of creation _____.
    A. should be taken literally
    B. makes sense
    C. should be taken symbolically
    D. is compatible with science

4. According to the Big Bang theory, there was _____ before the big explosion.
    A. nothing
    B. matter
    C. a black hole
    D. a black hole and matter

5. Material education is concerned with _____.
    A. the physical body and material aspects of man
    B. the development of the capacities within human intellect and mind
    C. the development of the divine qualities within an individual
    D. A and B only

6. The Big Bang happened when _____.
    A. two planets crashed into each other
    B. there was a nuclear explosion
    C. matter was crushed
    D. finite matter acquired infinite density under infinite pressure

7. The Big Bang theory _____ where the initial matter came from.
    A. explains
    B. does not explain
    C. shows
    D. none of the above

8. The Big Bang theory _____ the source of laws governing the process of birth of stars.
    A. explains
    B. does not explain
    C. shows
    D. none of the above

9. The birth and death of stars and galaxies _____.
    A. is a continuous process
    B. happened only once during the Big Bang
    C. is a very rare event
    D. none of the above

10. A new star is created _____.
    A. from a combination of other planets
    B. from fusion of matter
    C. when a dying star explodes
    D. none of the above

11. The physical world _____.
    A. has a beginning
    B. has no beginning
    C. has died and emerged many times
    D. none of the above

12. The physical world _____.
    A. will end sometime in the future
    B. will end and be reborn in the future
    C. is eternal
    D. none of the above

13. The theory of creation has been _____.
    A. scientifically proven
    B. shown to be true beyond doubt
    C. is just a theory and not proven

D. none of the above

1.4.2 Short-answer questions

1. Explain why the story of creation described in the Bible should be taken symbolically not literally.

   _____
   _____
   _____
   _____
   _____
   _____

2. Explain briefly the Big Bang theory.

   _____
   _____
   _____
   _____
   _____
   _____

3. Does the physical world have a beginning? Explain.

   _____
   _____
   _____
   _____

4. Does the earth have a beginning? Explain.

   _____
   _____
   _____
   _____

5. Could the physical world ever end? Explain.

   _____

_____
_____
_____

6. Could the earth ever end? Explain.

_____
_____
_____
_____

1.4.3 Projects

1. Illustrate the formation of our universe from the Big-Bang in a drawing.
2. Research the Big-Bang theory using the Internet. Focus on the following questions:
    a) What observations led to such a theory?
    b) Who were the first scientists who proposed the Big-Bang theory?
    c) What are the latest developments on the Big-Bang theory?

2 EVOLUTION OF THE UNIVERSE

2.1 Introduction

Ordinary matter is a building block of the universe and the main visible constituent of everything that exists in the physical world. It, however, constitutes only 4% of the universe, and the remainder is dark matter and dark energy. The definition and the model of matter has changed with increasing human scientific and technological understanding, and development. In this chapter, we study the latest theories about the structure and nature of matter. We will also explore how ordinary matter has evolved since the emergence of the universe. We look at both scientific and philosophical views on these issues.

In this chapter, you need to reflect on and understand the following key points:

a) Everything in the physical world is made out of matter.
b) The atom is the building block of matter.
c) An atom consists of a number of smaller particles.
d) Matter can exist in several different forms or phases, depending on the ambient temperature, pressure and volume.
e) In the beginning, all matter was one.
f) All natural forms of matter are the products of the on-going evolution of the universe since the Big Bang.
g) Evolution of matter has been occurring according to a "universal law" and "natural organisation"—designed by an intelligent Creator rather than driven by chaos and random processes.

2.2 Ordinary matter

The term matter traditionally refers to the visible substances that everything in the physical world is made of. It is usually defined by its physical properties as anything that has mass and volume. Scientifically, the concept of matter has been revised and evolved as man has developed a better understanding of the physical world.

2.2.1 Atomic structure of matter

Scientific discoveries show that physical matter is made up of atoms. A typical atom is about one millionth of a millimetre across. In other words, a million atoms laid in a line would measure one millimetre across.

Each atom itself consists of electrons, protons and neutrons that interact with each other. More recent discoveries have shown that protons and neutrons are composite particles composed of elementary particles called quarks.

2.2.2 Different phases of matter

Atoms are held together by electromagnetic forces. Matter can exist in several different forms or phases, depending on the ambient temperature, pressure and volume. The most common phases of matter include solids, liquids and gases. There are also more complex phases such as plasmas, superfluids, supersolids, etc. Matter changes from one phase to another when ambient conditions change.

Scientists now believe that ordinary matter constitutes only about 4% of the universe. The remainder consists of 23% dark matter and 73% dark energy.

Dark matter does not emit or reflect sufficient electromagnetic radiation to be directly observed and its composition is unknown. Dark energy is the name given to the antigravity influence that is accelerating the rate of the expansion of the universe.

Particle physics also identifies antimatter that is composed of the antiparticles of those that constitute ordinary matter. If a particle and its antiparticle should come into contact with each other, they instantly convert to energy. Antimatter does not exist naturally on the earth.

2.3 Evolution of matter in the universe

Scientific discoveries indicate that all natural forms of matter are the products of the on-going evolution of the universe since the Big Bang. The initial creation of matter was from light elements within a few minutes after the Big Bang. This evolution has continued towards emergence of lighter matter.

In Some Answered Questions, 'Abdu'l-Bahá sheds further light on the evolution of the universe and matter. He states, *"... in the beginning matter was one, and that one matter appeared in different aspects in each element. Thus various forms were produced, and these various aspects as they were produced became permanent, and each element was specialized. But this permanence was not definite, and did not attain realization and perfect existence until after a very long time. Then these elements became composed, and organized and combined in infinite forms; or rather from the composition and combination of these elements innumerable beings appeared."*[1]

The process has been occurring according to a "universal law" and "natural organisation" designed by an intelligent Creator rather than driven by chaos and random processes. The original embryonic matter consisted of elements in their earlier forms. They all gradually developed and passed from one shape and form to another over many ages and cycles. The result is the perfect world and system that we now witness.

The process of evolution of matter is similar to the growth of the human embryo in the womb of the mother. The process begins with one cell that rapidly starts to multiply after conception. It then evolves through different forms and conditions until it reaches the perfect shape of a human being.

Another example is the growth of the seed of a flower. In the beginning it looks very small and insignificant. However, it grows in the womb of the earth and evolves through different forms and shapes until it appears in the perfect condition of a flower.

Similarly, the original matter of the universe started to expand and develop within the matrix of the universe after its original emergence. It has evolved through different forms and shapes to reach its current condition.

---

[1] 'Abdu'l-Bahá, *Some Answered Questions*, p. 181.

Since the whole universe operates under one natural system, the structure, organisation and operation of the atom, as the smallest entity in matter, resembles the organisation, structure and operation of the galaxies.

2.4 Who is 'Abdu'l-Bahá?

In section 2.3 the concept of the evolution of matter as described by 'Abdu'l-Bahá was cited. Further references will be given in the following chapters regarding the philosophical concepts and ideas described by 'Abdu'l-Bahá in His Writings. It is important to know more about 'Abdu'l-Bahá to appreciate the significance of the views expressed by Him. Hence, a brief introduction to the life and philosophy of 'Abdu'l-Bahá is given in this section.

'Abdu'l-Bahá was the son of Bahá'u'lláh, the Prophet Founder of the Bahá'í Faith. He was born on 23 May 1844 and passed away on 28 November 1921. He was appointed by Bahá'u'lláh as His successor, the interpreter of His Writings, and the Centre of His Covenant. 'Abdu'l-Bahá wrote a number of books and numerous letters that are known as Tablets.

'Abdu'l-Bahá wrote extensively on philosophical issues and He provided novel and interesting concepts regarding fundamental questions asked in philosophy such as: the origin of the universe, the nature of man and life after death.

The concepts described by 'Abdu'l-Bahá shed new light on these complicated issues. Hence, we often refer to them in this book.

2.5 Activities
2.5.1 Multiple choice questions

1. Matter is _____.
    A. the solid material found on earth
    B. the substance the physical world is made of
    C. the substance available only under the ground
    D. none of the above

2. The building block of matter is _____.
    A. the atom
    B. the molecule
    C. the proton
    D. none of the above

3. A typical atom is about _____ long.
    A. a millimetre
    B. one hundredth of a millimetre
    C. one millionth of a millimetre
    D. None of the above

4. Different phases of matter are produced under varying ambient _____.
    A. temperatures
    B. pressures
    C. volumes
    D. all of the above

5. Different phases of matter include _____.
    A. solids
    B. liquids
    C. gases
    D. all of the above

6. Ordinary matter constitutes about _____ of the observable universe.
    A. 0.4%
    B. 4%
    C. 40%
    D. 100%

7. Dark matter _____.

A. is black
   B. can be seen only during the day
   C. is invisible
   D. none of the above

8. Dark energy is _____ of matter.
   A. the gravity force
   B. the anti-gravity
   C. electromagnetic force
   D. none of the above

9. In the beginning of the universe, matter was _____.
   A. one
   B. diversified
   C. in the form of different types of gases
   D. none of the above

10. The evolution and multiplication of matter has been according to _____.
    A. a natural organisation
    B. a universal law
    C. an intelligent design
    D. all of the above

11. The physical world _____.
    A. has a beginning
    B. has no beginning
    C. has died and emerged many times
    D. none of the above

12. The evolution of matter resembles _____.
    A. the growth of human embryo in the womb
    B. growth of the seed of a flower in the matrix of the earth
    C. both of the above
    D. none of the above

13. The smallest particle of an atom is _____.
    A. the electron
    B. the proton
    C. the neutron
    D. None of the above

2.5.2 Short-answer questions

1. Briefly describe your understanding of the following:

   a) Ordinary matter

   _____
   _____
   _____
   _____

   b) Dark matter

   _____
   _____
   _____
   _____

   c) Dark energy

   _____
   _____
   _____
   _____

2. Briefly describe different phases of matter.

   _____
   _____
   _____
   _____

3. Briefly describe the evolution of matter since the Big Bang.

   _____
   _____
   _____
   _____
   _____

4. Provide an analogy to illustrate the evolution of matter.

5. Compare the structure and organisation of an atom and the solar system.

2.5.3 Projects

1. Look for some photos and images on the Internet that illustrate the evolution of galaxies and matter.
2. Conduct a search on the Internet to obtain information about the "periodic table" of basic elements. How does this table illustrate the evolution of matter?
3. Search for the major Writings of 'Abdu'l-Bahá on the Internet.

3 Emergence of Life

3.1 Introduction

The nature of the emergence of life on the earth has been another burning question on the mind of man over many millennia. Many religions have explained the origin and nature of life according to the understanding of people of their time. Philosophers and scientists have also been working hard to explain the origin of life using rational methods and scientific experiments.

In this chapter, we initially reflect on life and its nature, and try to distinguish it from lifeless matter. We then briefly look at the materialistic view regarding the emergence of life. In the final part of the chapter, we will study a holistic view on the emergence of life and the universe as explained by 'Abdu'l-Bahá.

In this chapter, you need to reflect on and understand the following key points:

a) An object has life when it exhibits self-sustaining biological processes.
b) The structural unit of all known living organisms is known as the "cell".
c) The cell is also a unit of function, reproduction and heredity characteristics in all living organisms.
d) There is no scientifically proven model for the origin of life on the earth.
e) According to 'Abdu'l-Bahá, life emerged as the result of the interaction between Spirit and matter.
f) Spirit or Love is the animating power from God that flows through the universe.

g) There is life in other parts of the universe.

3.2 Life

An object has life when it exhibits self-sustaining biological processes. Some examples of biological processes are digestion and reproduction. Life is a process that unfolds in different forms in the Universe. The structural unit of all known living organisms is known as "cell". This is the smallest unit that is classified as living. The cell is also a unit of function, reproduction and heredity characteristics in living organism.

Living organisms may be composed of a single free cell or composed of masses of cells. New cells are always derived from existing cells through a process of division. A cell can grow, divide and die independent of the surrounding cells in the organism. Genetic information is stored and expressed within the cells and passed from one generation to another in the cells.

In the first half of the 20th century, scientists assumed that the cell was a fairly simple entity. It was treated as a black box that mysteriously performed complex functions. Using the technologies that have emerged over the last few decades such as electronic microscope, scientists have discovered the complexity of the cell.

3.3 Origin and source of life

Within the natural sciences, a great effort has been made to find the origin of life on the earth. It is obvious that at some point life emerged from lifeless matter. The first living things on the earth are thought to have been single cells without a nucleus. The oldest ancient fossil microbe-like objects discovered are 3 billion years old.

Despite extensive research, science has not been able to identify the exact sequence of events that led to the appearance of the first life on the earth. All attempts to synthesize a live cell based on components that would have the necessary properties of life have proved inconclusive. Hence, there is no scientifically proven model of the origin of life on the earth.

The failure of science to understand and reproduce life may be an indication that a materialistic approach is not adequate to explain life. Similar to many mystical processes that we encounter in the physical world, life seems to have a spiritual dimension in addition to the physical one.

'Abdu'l-Bahá provides a spiritual explanation of life based on matter and Spirit.[1] According to Him, creation of life is a self-perpetuating process that has neither a beginning nor an end. This is how the process takes place:

- Matter, as discussed in chapter one, is eternal and fills all of space.
- Spirit or Love, which reflects the positive and active aspects of God, flows in the universe and passes through the matter.
- Through the interaction with matter, Spirit marks its properties and nature on the atoms and elements of matter.
- This interaction unites the atoms and elements according to certain laws and brings into existence the worlds, galaxies and everything else in the physical world.
- Under the appropriate conditions, the interaction of Spirit with matter in a similar process creates life.

Spirit is the animating power from God that constantly flows through the universe, creating the physical world and bringing life into existence. The meaning of Spirit in this context is different from the usual meaning given to the word "spirit" that refers to the soul and spirituality. The Spirit or energy animating animals and humanity is referred to by 'Abdu'l-Bahá as the "force of life".[2]

3.4 Life in the universe

So far, scientific observations have not discovered any life beyond the earth. However, Bahá'u'lláh in one of His Tablets makes an amazing statement about life on other planets. He states: "... *every fixed star hath its own planets, and every planet its own creatures, whose number no man can compute.*"[3]

As studied in the previous section, 'Abdu'l-Bahá explains that under appropriate conditions, the interaction of Spirit with matter creates life. Based on these two concepts expressed by Bahá'u'lláh and 'Abdu'l-Bahá, we may conclude that life will emerge on a planet when the right conditions prevail.

---

[1] 'Abdu'l-Bahá, *Bahá'í Scriptures*, p. 301.
[2] 'Abdu'l-Bahá, *The Promulgation of Universal Peace*, p. 317.
[3] Bahá'u'lláh, *Gleanings from the Writings of Bahá'u'lláh*, p. 162.

The right conditions on a planet come into existence through evolution of matter on that planet, similar to what has taken place on the earth.

3.5 Who is Bahá'u'lláh?

In section 3.4 we read a statement from Bahá'u'lláh about the life on other planets. There will be more references in the coming chapters regarding the concepts described by Bahá'u'lláh in His Writings. It is important to know Who Bahá'u'lláh is to appreciate the significance of His Writings. Hence, an introduction to Bahá'u'lláh is provided in this section.

The life of Bahá'u'lláh is one of the most extraordinary stories of this age. Bahá'u'lláh is the Prophet Founder of the Bahá'í Faith. As the son of a minister in the court of the king of Írán, He was born into a wealthy family on 12 November 1817 and was brought up in comfort and abundance. He declared that He was the latest Manifestation of God (or Prophet) and receiver of a new Revelation. Many people accepted His claim and followed His teachings.

The authorities and clergy of that time felt threatened by Bahá'u'lláh, and, consequently, in order to stop the progress of His religion, they arrested and imprisoned Him, and then exiled Him to foreign lands, where he survived the remaining 40 years of his life. However, this only encouraged the spread of the Bahá'í Faith. Bahá'u'lláh passed away on 29 May 1892 in Bahjí near 'Akká in Palestine (now Israel), the last place to which He was exiled.

The main goal of the Revelation of Bahá'u'lláh is to unite mankind on the earth. In His Writings, Bahá'u'lláh has provided humanity with a set of progressive teachings by which to achieve this goal.

3.6 Activities

3.6.1 Multiple choice questions

1. An object has life when it can _____.
   A. grow
   B. reproduce
   C. digest
   D. all of the above

2. The structure unit of a living organism is _____.
   A. the atom
   B. the molecule
   C. the cell
   D. None of the above

3. A living organism consists of _____.
   A. one cell
   B. multiple identical cells
   C. multiple different cells
   D. all of the above

4. In an organism, a cell _____ independently from the surrounding cells.
   A. cannot grow
   B. can divide
   C. does not die
   D. all of the above

5. Genetic information is passed on when the cell _____.
   A. divides
   B. grows
   C. dies
   D. all of the above

6. The first living things on the earth were _____.
   A. fish
   B. single cell organisms without a nucleus
   C. single cell organisms with a nucleus
   D. none of the above

7. Science has _____ the exact sequence of events that led to the appearance of the first life on the earth.

- A. discovered
- B. identified
- C. not discovered
- D. none of the above

8. There is _____ of the origin of life on the earth.
   - A. a scientific model
   - B. no scientific model
   - C. some scientific understanding
   - D. none of the above

9. Science has _____ to synthesise a live cell from raw material.
   - A. valid theories on how
   - B. been able
   - C. not been able
   - D. none of the above

10. The failure of science to understand life is an indication that _____.
    - A. life has a spiritual dimension
    - B. science has not taken the right approach
    - C. science is in its infancy
    - D. None of the above

11. Spirit mentioned by 'Abdu'l-Bahá _____.
    - A. reflects the positive and active aspect of God
    - B. is the same as Love
    - C. is the animating and life giving energy from God
    - D. all of the above

12. Spirit creates life _____ .
    - A. when the matter has the right atomic structure
    - B. when there is a cell available
    - C. through interaction with the atoms of matter
    - D. none of the above

13. There is _____ in other parts of the universe.
    - A. life
    - B. human life
    - C. no life
    - D. none of the above

3.6.2 Short-answer questions

1. What are the main characteristics of a living entity?

2. What is the structural unit of a living entity? What functions does this unit perform?

3. Explain why a spiritual component is necessary to create life.

4. How does life emerge from matter according to 'Abdu'l-Bahá?

5. Is there life in other galaxies? Explain the reason.

3.6.3 Projects

1. Conduct a search on the Internet for at least two scientific theories on the origin of life on the earth.
2. What are the latest scientific discoveries regarding the existence of life on other planets. Provide a summary.
3. Prepare a poster to illustrate the interaction between Spirit and matter in producing life.
4. Compile a list of the social teachings of Bahá'u'lláh.

4 Diversity of Life on Earth

4.1 Introduction

In the physical world, life emerges in different forms. A cell, as the basic structural and functional unit of life, has a specific composition and structure depending on its type. In this chapter, we look at the diversity of life within an organism and also in the physical world. Life in an organism has a hierarchy that starts with the cell and extends to encompass the complete organism. In the physical world on the earth, we identify four different levels of existence or kingdoms; the mineral, the vegetable, the animal and the human. We will discuss the powers and abilities associated with each kingdom.

In this chapter, you need to reflect on and understand the following key points:

a) In the physical world, life emerges in different forms.
b) Within each organism, there is a hierarchy of life, starting with the cell and extending to encompass the complete organism.
c) In the physical world on the earth, we identify four different levels of existence or kingdoms: the mineral, the vegetable, the animal and the human.
d) The power associated with the mineral kingdom is "cohesion".
e) The powers associated with the vegetable kingdom are "cohesion" and "growth".
f) The powers associated with the animal kingdom are "cohesion", "growth" and "sensory perception".
g) The powers associated with the human kingdom are "cohesion", "growth", "sensory perception" and "reasoning".

4.2 Hierarchy of Life

In the physical world, life emerges in different forms. The cell, as discussed in chapter 3, is the basic structural and functional unit of life. The composition and structure of cells depends on their functions. For example, the cell in a single cell organism is significantly different from the cells in a complex animal such as a bird.

The cells constituting an organ unite in clusters to form the different tissues associated with that organ. The tissues in the organ work collectively to perform the function expected of that organ. For example, all the tissues in the heart of the bird have the one aim of pumping blood through to other organs in the body. This is illustrated in Figure 4.1.

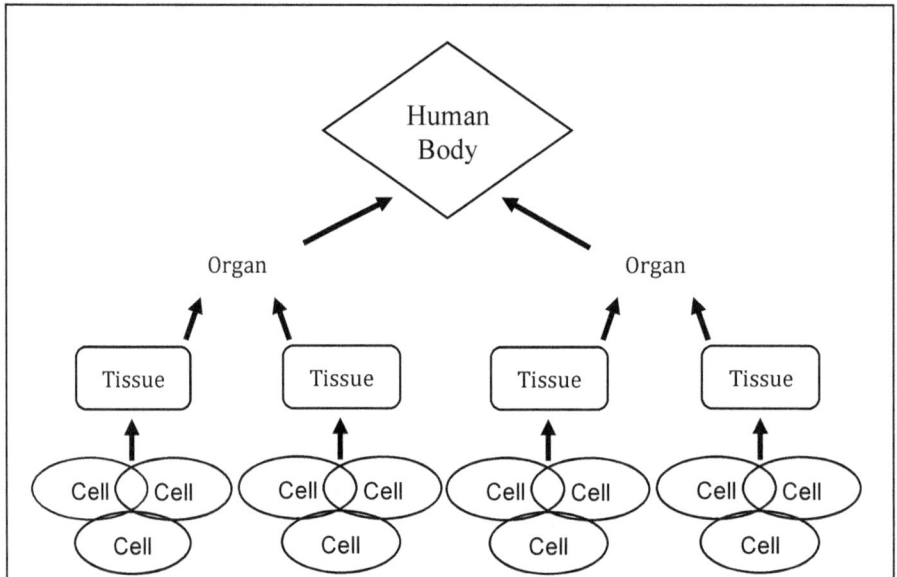

Figure 4.1 – Illustration of the hierarchy of human life

The organs in the body of the bird operate continuously and in unison to give the bird the life characteristics that it manifests, such as the ability to digest food, move, grow and reproduce.

This organisation can be called the hierarchy of life. This concept can be extended to include socio-environmental organisations that exist on our planet. For example, all the different types of birds can be considered as a class of the population of animals, the Aves. The collection of all species living on earth can be considered as the community of living creatures. This community co-exists and interacts with the environment that collectively is called the ecosystem.

It is obvious that higher levels of life exist when the lower levels thrive and remain intact. A higher level also manifests characteristics not found in the lower levels.

4.3 Categories of existence

The physical world of existence on the earth can be divided into four categories or kingdoms according to the characteristics and properties that each category demonstrates. They are: the mineral, the vegetable, the animal and the human.[1] The following sections will explain more about each category.

4.3.1 Mineral Kingdom

This category includes all lifeless matter as described in chapter 2. The basis of the whole physical system is built from this material. As mentioned before, the atoms and particles of matter are held together through electromagnetic forces. This is called the power of *"cohesion"*. Hence, the dominant characteristic of entities in this kingdom is the attraction between their particles or "cohesion". For example, a chair appears as a chair because the particles forming the chair stick together to form its shape and physical characteristics. Without cohesion, the physical world would not exist.

4.3.2 Vegetable Kingdom

This category includes every living thing that generally does not move bodily or independently, and is known as vegetation, including fungi, algae and multi-cellular plants such as trees, flowers, grasses etc. The building element of species in the vegetable kingdom is matter. Hence, members of the vegetable kingdom have the power of cohesion. However, they demonstrate some new characteristics that are absent in the mineral kingdom. All the entities in the vegetable kingdom have the ability to grow and reproduce. For example, a chair can neither grow nor reproduce another chair under any circumstances. However, a tree grows from a tiny seed. It produces a trunk, branches, twigs, leaves, roots, flowers and new seeds that can produce new trees.

---

[1] This concept is described by 'Abdu'l-Bahá in one of His Tablets published in *The Promulgation of Universal peace*, p. 258.

4.3.3 Animal Kingdom

The third category, the animal kingdom, embraces all the other living species on the earth apart from man. The physical body of animals is also made out of matter and hence it has the power of cohesion. Animals also grow and reproduce. However, they manifest a new power that is absent in the vegetable kingdom.

Animals have a central brain that communicates through a nervous system with the body of the animal. It receives sensory information from the five senses of vision, touch, smell, hearing and taste. The brain processes the information, and issues appropriate commands to drive various muscles to interact with the environment. This is known as the power of sensory perception.

In summary, members of the animal kingdom have the powers of cohesion, growth, as well as the ability to sense their environment through five sense organs.

4.3.4 Human Kingdom

The human kingdom has all the powers of the mineral, vegetable and animal kingdoms. Our bodies are made out of matter. We can grow physically and can reproduce. We have the five basic senses of animals and can interact with our physical environment by processing the information that we receive from our sensors. In addition, we have the ability to reason based on abstract thought and to make decisions. This is known as the rational, logical or reasoning power.

Using this power, we can discover previously unknown information by reasoning applied to observations obtained from our senses. The discoveries and inventions of human science and technology are the products of the human rational power.

The various kingdoms and the powers manifested by them are illustrated in Figure 4.2.

4.4 Animating power in each kingdom

In chapter 3, we mentioned that life appears as the Spirit, or Love, flows in the universe and passes through matter. Through its interaction with matter, Spirit stamps its properties and nature on the atoms and elements of matter. Under the appropriate conditions and to the extent of the refinement of matter, different degrees of life emerge and corresponding powers are manifested. The Spirit, provides the energy and animating power required for each kingdom. For example, in vegetable kingdom, the Spirit creates the characteristics of cohesion and growth, in the animal the extra power of sensory perception and in the human the power of reasoning. When the Spirit acts on the human body, it is known as the "human spirit". This is different from the human soul, which represents the identity of an individual as will be explained in section 9.3.

	Mineral	Vegetable	Animal	Human
Kingdom				
Powers	Cohesion	Cohesion Growth	Cohesion Growth Sensory	Cohesion Growth Sensory Reasoning

Figure 4.2 – Different kingdoms and their powers

4.5 Activities

4.5.1 Multiple choice questions

1. All the cells in an organism _____.
   A. are identical
   B. vary according to each organ
   C. vary according to the tissues in each organ
   D. None of the above

2. The cells constituting an organ unite in clusters forming _____.
   A. different tissues of the organ
   B. the organ
   C. the organism
   D. None of the above

3. The tissues in an organ work collectively to _____.
   A. keep the organ alive
   B. receive nutrients from the blood stream
   C. perform the function expected from that organ
   D. all of the above

4. By ecosystem is meant _____.
   A. the environment
   B. the collection of all the species on the earth
   C. the coexistence of all the species on the earth and the environment
   D. none of the above

5. _____ is (are) the unique characteristic(s) of the mineral kingdom.
   A. Cohesiveness
   B. Cohesiveness and growth
   C. Cohesiveness, growth and reproduction
   D. Cohesiveness, growth, reproduction and sensory perception

6. _____ is (are) the unique characteristic(s) of the vegetable kingdom.
   A. Cohesiveness
   B. Cohesiveness and growth
   C. Cohesiveness, growth and reproduction
   D. Cohesiveness, growth, reproduction and sensory perception

7. _____ is (are) the unique characteristic(s) of the animal kingdom.
   A. Cohesiveness
   B. Cohesiveness and growth
   C. Cohesiveness, growth and reproduction
   D. Cohesiveness, growth, reproduction, and sensory perception

8. The main difference between the human kingdom and the animal kingdom is _____.
   A. sensory perception
   B. power of cohesion
   C. power of reasoning
   D. none of the above

9. The main difference between the animal kingdom and the vegetable kingdom is _____.
   A. sensory perception
   B. power of cohesion
   C. power of reasoning
   D. none of the above

10. The main difference between the vegetable kingdom and the mineral kingdom is _____.
    A. sensory perception
    B. power of cohesion
    C. power of reasoning
    D. none of the above

11. The characteristics of each kingdom is produced as the result of _____.
    A. the Spirit acting on matter
    B. purification of matter
    C. evolution of matter
    D. none of the above

12. The central brain can be found only _____.
    A. in the vegetable kingdom
    B. in animals
    C. in humans and animals
    D. none of the above

13. Sensory perception is produced through _____.

    A. the power of reasoning
    B. processing of sensory information by the brain
    C. the power of decision making
    D. None of the above
14. Humans can discover unknowns through _____.
    A. the power of reasoning
    B. processing of sensory information by the brain
    C. the power of decision making
    D. none of the above

4.5.2 Short-answer questions

1. What is your understanding of the life hierarchy?

_____
_____
_____
_____
_____
_____
_____
_____
_____

2. What is the ecosystem?

_____
_____
_____
_____

3. What is the mineral kingdom?

_____
_____
_____
_____

4. What is the main property of the mineral kingdom? Explain.

_____

5. What is the vegetable kingdom?

6. What are the main properties of the vegetable kingdom? Explain.

7. What is the animal kingdom?

8. What is the main property of the animal kingdom? Explain.

9. What is the human kingdom?

10. What is the main property of the human kingdom? Explain.

_____
_____
_____
_____

11. What is your understanding of the human spirit?

_____
_____
_____
_____

4.5.3 Projects

1. Prepare a poster to illustrate the life hierarchy described in section 4.2.
2. Some plants respond to stimuli. Conduct some research to demonstrate the differences between the way plants sense stimuli and the sensory perception of animals.
3. Reflect on how you make decisions. Write down the steps you take in your decision making. Provide an example.

5 EVOLUTION OF LIFE ON EARTH

5.1 Introduction

It is now scientifically proven that the diverse organisms currently living on the earth have undergone changes and transformations to evolve over a long period of time. This process of change is known as the evolution of life. In this chapter we shall explore the concept of evolution and attempt to distinguish between the facts and theories surrounding this concept. We will show that it is possible to conclude that man has always been a distinct, original species, uniquely different from other animals although sharing aspects of their physical appearance in the earlier stages of prehistory.

In this chapter, you need to reflect on and understand the following key points:

a) The term "evolution" implies the mechanism that drives variations in a species.
b) The term "evolution" is sometimes used to convey the concept of "common descent"—this implies that all creatures on earth descended from the same ancestor.
c) Charles Darwin suggests that the evolution of organisms has occurred through "natural selection".
d) In modern evolutionary theories, any variation in DNA and genetic code from one generation to another is also considered to be a mechanism driving the evolution of organisms.
e) The apparent appearance of the animal kingdom before the human kingdom does not necessarily mean that man was raised from the animal world.

f) Even if we assume that at some stage man walked on "all fours" or had a tail, man has always been a distinct species from other animals.

5.2 Concept of evolution

Scientific observations and experiments indicate that the genetic structure and characteristics of an organism can change over time from one generation to the next due to various factors. This is known as the evolution of organisms and has been frequently observed in laboratory studies of some simple organisms.

In scientific and philosophical writings, the term "evolution" has also been used in reference to two related but distinct ideas: the concept of common descent and the mechanisms that drive variation in a species. These concepts will be studied in the following sections.

5.2.1 Common descent

The concept of "common descent" implies that all creatures on the earth come from the same ancestor. This is an old concept that goes back to ancient Greek philosophers such as Anaximander. He believed that life had emerged from matter and that man had evolved from animals.

An English naturalist, Charles Robert Darwin (12 February 1809—19 April 1882), extended this old concept by suggesting that such evolution has occurred through a mechanism called "natural selection". He published his findings in 1859 in a book called *On the Origin of Species*.

According to Darwin's theory, life has emerged from matter and has constantly changed. In this process new species have emerged through divergence from and transformation of older species. The large differences currently observed in different species are the result of many small incremental changes that have occurred over a very long period of time. There is a great deal of controversy about these ideas since the details of these processes have not been scientifically verified, and all the structural differences observed between species cannot be proved to have their origins from the accumulation of many small incremental variations.

Darwin also suggests that all members of a species vary slightly from each other as indicated by their different structural, behavioural, and physiological traits. Such differences enable some organisms to adapt better to their environment and to eventually pass their beneficial traits on to future generations. Over a long period of time, the accumulating effect of these small changes results in the emergence of a new species. The whole process is known as "natural selection" or the "survival of the fittest." Thus, according to Darwin's theory, natural selection occurs as a result of individual organisms, which are better adapted to a changing environment, having a better survival rate and time to pass on their genes.

For example, some scientists suggest that at some stage giraffes had shorter necks. Those born with a longer-than-normal neck had a feeding advantage in being able to reach higher foliage, especially during times of intense competition for food, drought, or other environmental changes. With a greater ability to survive came more opportunities to reproduce and pass on their "longer neck" genes. Hence, over a long period of time the modern long-necked giraffe evolved.

However, two scientists in Africa recently noted that giraffes spent most of the dry season, when food was scarce, feeding on low bushes; and during the rainy season the giraffes were able to feed on the abundant green leaves of tall trees. They proposed the long necks developed as a result of competition with other males, where the long and heavy necks are used as a weapon, for the right to reproduce.

5.2.2 Mechanisms of evolution

In modern evolutionary theories, it is proposed that besides natural selection, the genetic variations caused by the interaction between changes in the genetic code and the environment also drives the evolution of organisms.

Genetics is a modern field of biology that studies how the traits of parents are passed on to offspring. The genetic information is held in structures called chromosomes within the nucleus of a cell. Chromosomes are made up of long strands of a chemical called deoxyribonucleic acid (DNA). The genetic information in the DNA is organised in the form of coded instructions called genes. Our genes contain all the information required to make a distinct human being.

Naturally occurring variations of the genetic code, such as mutations and genetic drift, can be scientifically observed between different generations of a species.

5.3 Evolution and man

There is no doubt that everything in nature evolves, including matter and life. However, to assume that man is descended from an animal is an unreasonable conclusion. In this section, we look at two arguments made by the supporters of the concept of "common descent".

The earth is over 4.5 billion years old and life started on it about 3.8 billion years ago with the appearance of single-celled organisms. Life as we know it today appeared 570 million years ago—starting with arthropods, then fish 530 million, land plants 475 million, trees 385 million, and mammals 200 million years ago. The first modern humans, known as *Homo sapiens*, only appeared 200,000 years ago.

Darwinists argue that because of the relatively late emergence of modern man, it must be the result of his evolution from other animals such as the great apes that share many physical similarities. However, if the evolution time argument is used to conclude that man evolved from apes then, based on the same time argument, we should also believe that land plants evolved from fish who preceded them on the evolutionary time scale. Neither of these assumptions are correct. But, the scientist might argue, land plants are nothing at all like fish! That might sound like a reasonable objection for those that believe that, just because of some superficial physical similarities to apes, humans are only another species of the animal kingdom. In reality, in the most important aspects of their being, both spiritual and intellectual, humans are so very different from the apes, that they must belong to a separate kingdom. Hence, the appearance of the animal kingdom before the human kingdom does not necessarily mean that man evolved from the animal world.[1]

A further comment should be made with regard to the similarity of the physical features of early humans to apes. This similarity during human physical evolution does not necessarily indicate that humankind has evolved from the animal kingdom. Even if at some stage human beings walked on all fours or had a tail, man has always belonged to a distinct kingdom from the animals with his own special powers as explained in section 4.3 .

---

[1] 'Abdu'l-Bahá, *Some Answered Questions*, p. 192.

The development of the human embryo in the womb is a good example of how the human form evolves through different physical stages. The embryo changes from form to form and shape to shape until it becomes a human foetus with a distinctly human form at about 10 weeks of intrauterine life. At one stage in its mother's womb, the human embryo looks like a worm and later like a frog. However, through all these stages, and regardless of its physical appearance, this embryo is a human being, and it can never develop into anything other than a human being. Similarly, man has evolved in the matrix of the world as a unique species distinctly different from animals and has gradually evolved from one physical form to another to reach his present appearance.[1]

Hence, even if science can prove that human ancestors had an appearance similar to various animals at some stage of their evolution, mankind remains distinctly different from the animal kingdom.

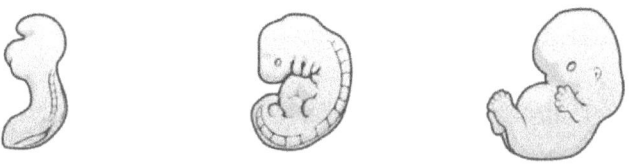

Figure 5.1 – Illustration of the development of human embryo

---

[1] 'Abdu'l-Bahá, *Some Answered Questions*, p. 193.

5.4 Activities
5.4.1 Multiple choice questions
1. Diverse organisms currently living on the earth have _____.
   A. always been in existence
   B. have evolved over time
   C. have all suddenly come into existence at the same time
   D. none of the above
2. The genetic structure and characteristics of an organism _____.
   A. can change over time from one generation to the next
   B. is fixed
   C. can change during the lifetime of an organism
   D. none of the above
3. Evolution means _____.
   A. a change in the genetic structure
   B. absorbing nutrients present the blood
   C. performing the function expected of that organ
   D. all of the above
4. Evolution refers to _____.
   A. a change in the genetic structure
   B. the mechanism driving the change
   C. the concept of "common descent"
   D. all of the above
5. The concept of evolution _____.
   A. was proposed in the 18th century
   B. was proposed in the 19th century
   C. goes back to the ancient Greeks
   D. none of the above
6. According to Darwin's theory of evolution, life _____.
   A. has no beginning
   B. has emerged from lifeless matter
   C. has different sources
   D. none of the above
7. According to Darwin, large differences currently observed in different species are the result of _____.

A. small incremental changes over a long period of time
B. rapid changes over a short period of time
C. random changes
D. none of the above

8. Darwin's theory of the incremental changes in the evolution of species _____.
   A. is scientifically proved as all changes have been identified
   B. is not scientifically proved as all the changes have not been identified
   C. is open to question as there are no changes in organisms
   D. none of the above

9. According to Darwin, all the members of a species _____ in structure, behaviour and physiological traits.
   A. are identical
   B. are vastly different
   C. vary slightly
   D. none of the above

10. According to Darwin's theory of "Natural Selection", different organisms _____.
    A. select a particular environment for their development
    B. select a particular way to evolve
    C. select a particular genetic structure
    D. do not actively select anything

11. The concept of "Natural Selection" is _____ the concept of "survival of the fittest".
    A. the same as
    B. different from
    C. a subset of
    D. none of the above

12. Modern man appeared _____ the emergence of other species.
    A. before
    B. after
    C. at the same time
    D. none of the above

13. The appearance of man _____ other organisms does not necessarily mean that man _____ evolved from the animal kingdom.
    A. before; has
    B. before; has not
    C. after; has
    D. after; has not

14. The physical similarity of man to some animals during his evolution _____ that man has evolved from the animal kingdom.
    A. must indicate
    B. does not necessary indicate
    C. has been proved to indicate
    D. none of the above

15. Man _____ other animals.
    A. has always been a distinct species from
    B. has evolved from
    C. is identical to
    D. none of the above

5.4.2 Short-answer questions

1. Describe the three meanings of the term "evolution" as defined in this chapter.

    _____
    _____
    _____
    _____

2. List in bullet form the main points of Darwin's theory of evolution.

    _____
    _____
    _____
    _____
    _____
    _____

3. Explain why there is controversy regarding Darwin's theory of how the multiplication and evolution of organisms have occurred through incremental changes over a long period of time.

_____
_____
_____
_____
_____
_____
_____
_____

4. Explain the concept of "Natural Selection".

_____
_____
_____
_____
_____
_____
_____
_____

5.4.3 Projects
1. Through research on the Internet, find out how the genetic code can change from one generation to another.
2. Design a poster to illustrate the geological timeline of the earth and mark periods where major forms of life (phylum or division) appeared on the earth. Use information that is available on the Internet.
3. Develop an argument to show that humankind has evolved in the matrix of the world as a unique entity distinctly different from the animal kingdom.

Section II – The nature of human beings

6 REALITY OF MAN

6.1 Introduction

In this chapter we will study human reality—the true essence and nature of man. We shall build on the concept of the hierarchy of life and explore how the behaviour of man at the macroscopic level of life as a complete individual is much more complex than the sum of the activities and characteristics of the atoms, cells and organs constituting that individual. In order to understand human reality, we shall develop a logical model based on the characteristics and behaviour exhibited by man. According to this model, human reality consists of three dimensions: the physical, intellectual and spiritual realities.

In this chapter, you need to reflect on and understand the following key points:

a) Human reality refers to the nature and state of actual existence of a human being.
b) The atoms and cells of an individual represent the microscopic characteristics of human reality.
c) The entire human body, on the other hand, comprising head, neck, torso, limbs, and all the internal and external tissues and organs, including the brain, represents the macroscopic characteristics of human reality.
d) The behaviour of man at the macroscopic level is much more complex than the sum of the activities of atoms, cells and organs at the microscopic level.
e) The qualities observed in man suggest human reality has three dimensions: physical reality, intellectual reality and spiritual reality.

6.2 Complexity of human reality

The term '"reality" has different meanings. Literally, it means "real" and in a broad sense it includes everything that exists no matter whether it is observable, or just abstract and comprehensible. Reality also refers to the state of actual existence, as distinct from imagination, fiction or pretence. This is an existence that has a purpose and is more than just an idea.

Human reality refers to a state of actual existence as well as the nature and essence of a human being. It answers questions like what we are, what is the purpose of our physical life, how and why we behave and live as we do, and why we are so different from animals.

In chapter 4, the concept of the hierarchy of life was introduced. The atoms and cells form the lowest level of this hierarchy can be considered as the microscopic level of man. The qualities of the entire human body, on the other hand, comprising head, neck, torso, limbs, and all the internal and external tissues and organs, including the brain, reflect the macroscopic level of man.

Human qualities at the macroscopic level are much more complex than the sum of the activities of atoms, cells and organs at the microscopic level. In fact, man exhibits characteristics and behaviour at the macroscopic scale for which there are no observable traces at the microscopic level.

For example, human intellectual abilities cannot be accurately located in any particular part of the human brain. The incredible capacity of man to process information and ponder over abstract thoughts has not been explained by our understanding of the human brain. In addition, emotions, artistic expressions and mystical feelings cannot be related to or explained by the function of any particular organ in the human body. Such characteristics are abstract and metaphysical, and are primarily observed and perceived conceptually.

The natural sciences have made astonishing progress over the last two centuries. They have acquired an accurate understanding of our biological and physiological composition and structure . Science can explain the most complex phenomena that occur at the microscopic level in the atoms and cells of man. Science can also describe the functions and operation of the organs in the human body, and the role of various chemicals flowing in the veins and arteries.

Since the qualities of human reality at the macroscopic level are at a higher level than the properties of physical matter, the natural sciences have not been able to understand or explain them. Many efforts in the social sciences have been made over the last two hundred years to accurately explain the dynamics and nature of human reality. However, no unified and accurate understanding has emerged. This can be attributed to two factors. The first is the abstract and non-tangible nature of human reality at the macroscopic level. The second is the extreme complexity of human reality. The concepts and theories that may describe human reality at the macroscopic scale are not as simple as those describing the operation and function of atoms and cells.

6.3 A Logical model for human reality

In this chapter, we develop a logical analysis of human reality based on the characteristics and behaviour exhibited by man. This model has been described by 'Abdu'l-Bahá in one of His utterances published in *Foundations of World Unity*.[1]

It was explained in chapter 3 that man has all the powers present in the mineral, vegetable and animal kingdoms. The human body is made out of matter and consequently has the power of cohesion. In addition, we grow, reproduce and have sensory perception. Collectively, we call such qualities or characteristics the outer or **physical reality** of man as they pertain to the physical existence of man and are also found in the animal kingdom.

We also understood in chapter 3 that man has the ability to reason and discover previously unknown information from already known information. This was referred to as the power of reasoning and represented a distinctive feature, differentiating man from the animal kingdom. We call this quality of man the **intellectual reality**.

Humankind exhibits other behaviours and characteristics that are radically different from what we can observe in the physical or intellectual realities. Experiencing mystical feelings has always been an integral part of the human life as shown by archaeological studies. The expression of feelings of devotion to God as the creator of the universe, in literature, as well as other arts such as music and painting, have become part of the treasure of human culture, and are clearly

---

[1] 'Abdu'l-Bahá, *Foundations of World Unity*, pp. 50–51.

different from discoveries and inventions made by science. Such qualities are the **spiritual reality** of man. Developing and practicing virtues, such as kindness and generosity, are also manifestations of the human spiritual reality.

The physical, intellectual and spiritual realities of man are all metaphysical and nonmaterial. Although they are different and independent, they interact and work hand in hand to form the human reality at the macroscopic level and create powers, abilities and characteristics reflecting the overall human nature and characteristics (see Figure 6.1).

For example, the three human realities provide man with a very complex perception system. The physical reality provides sensory perception by processing the information received from the sensory organs in the brain. The intellectual reality acts on the sensory perception and develops abstract thoughts through the power of reasoning of the mind. This is the intellectual perception. The human spiritual reality provides an alternative method for perception through the faculty of inner vision of the human soul. This is known as spiritual perception. These characteristics will be studied in the forthcoming chapters.

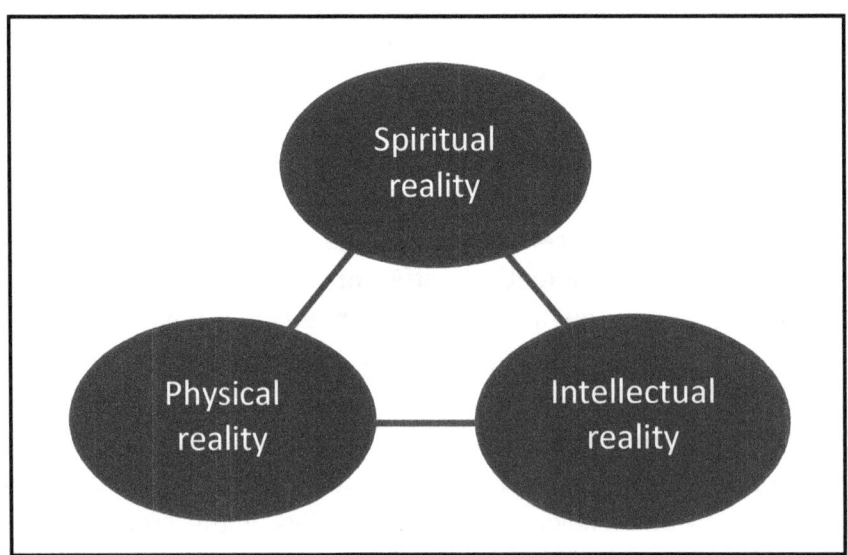

Figure 6.1 – The three dimensions of human reality

6.4 Activities

6.4.1 Multiple choice questions

1. The term reality can mean _____.
   A. real
   B. everything that is observable
   C. everything that is just abstract
   D. all of the above

2. The human reality means _____.
   A. the state of actual existence of a human being
   B. the nature and essence of a human being
   C. both of the above
   D. none of the above

3. The behaviour and characteristics of the _____ can be considered as the microscopic representation of the human reality.
   A. atoms and cells in the human body
   B. organs in the human body
   C. complete human body
   D. all of the above

4. The behaviour and characteristics of the _____ can be considered as the macroscopic representation of the human reality.
   A. atoms and cells in the human body
   B. organs in the human body
   C. complete human body
   D. all of the above

5. The human reality at macroscopic level _____ the sum of activities of the elements at the microscopic level.
   A. is equal to
   B. is much more than
   C. is less than
   D. all of the above

6. The human intellectual abilities _____.
   A. can be located in the brain
   B. cannot be located in the brain
   C. are spread in the brain and nerves

D. none of the above
7. The human artistic feelings are scientifically proven to relate to _____.
   A. the brain
   B. the heart
   C. all the organs
   D. none of the above
8. The natural sciences can explain complex phenomena that happen at _____ of the human reality.
   A. the microscopic level
   B. the macroscopic level
   C. both A and B
   D. none of the above
9. The social sciences can explain complex phenomena that happen at _____ of the human reality.
   A. the microscopic level
   B. the macroscopic level
   C. both A and B
   D. none of the above
10. There is _____ vision about the human reality at the macroscopic level as identified by social sciences.
    A. a unified
    B. a precise
    C. no unified
    D. none of the above
11. The human reality at the macroscopic level is _____.
    A. abstract
    B. non-tangible
    C. beyond matter
    D. all of the above
12. The human physical reality represents all the powers present in the _____.
    A. mineral kingdom
    B. vegetable kingdom
    C. animal kingdom
    D. all of the above

13. The human _____ reality can be identified by the power of reasoning.
    A. physical
    B. intellectual
    C. spiritual
    D. none of the above
14. The human _____ reality can be identified by mystical experiences.
    A. physical
    B. intellectual
    C. spiritual
    D. none of the above
15. The three realities of the human work _____.
    A. in isolation from each other
    B. hand in hand
    C. in pairs
    D. none of the above
16. The human _____ reality can be identified by the powers of cohesion, growth and sensory perception.
    A. physical
    B. intellectual
    C. spiritual
    D. none of the above
17. Practising virtues is a manifestation of the human _____ reality.
    A. physical
    B. intellectual
    C. spiritual
    D. none of the above

6.4.2 Short-answer questions

1. Describe your understanding of the term "human reality".

_____
_____
_____
_____

2. What are the microscopic and macroscopic scales of the human reality?

3. Why have the natural sciences been unable to explain the human reality at the macroscopic level?

4. Why have the social sciences been unable to provide a unified vision of the human reality at the macroscopic level?

5. What does the physical reality represent in man?

6. What does the intellectual reality represent in man?

_____
_____
_____
_____

7. What does the spiritual reality represent in man?

_____
_____
_____
_____

6.4.3 Projects

1. Reflect on yourself and identify the characteristics, behaviours and attributes that represent your physical, intellectual and spiritual realities. Design a poster showing the characteristics associated with each reality in separate lists.
2. Identify reasons and evidences that prove animals cannot have an intellectual reality.

7 HUMAN PHYSICAL REALITY

7.1 Introduction

So far, we have learned that man has all the faculties present in the mineral, vegetable and animal kingdoms. The human body is composed of matter and is formed as a coherent entity through the faculty of cohesion. Man can grow and reproduce, and possesses the power of sensory perception. In addition, the information in the DNA of our genes is the source of reactive responses known as instincts. Collectively, all these characteristics form our outer or physical reality. We will study the characteristics of the physical reality in this chapter.

In this chapter, you need to reflect on and understand the following key points:

a) Sensory perception provides man with an awareness of his environment.
b) In sensory perception, stimuli are received from the environment through specialised organs, and processed by brain cells in the cerebral cortex located at the rear of the brain.
c) Scientists have not been able to build a general-purpose computer that can display even the lowest degree of sensory perception.
d) Empirical evidence indicates that humans share common responses to certain stimuli from the time of their birth—these are known as instinctive behaviour.
e) The genes provide the instructions that give organisms their particular characteristics.
f) The behaviour of an animal is completely dictated by its instincts.

g) In man, some of the innate instincts observed in the newly born are lost as the infant grows. Otherwise the basic instincts of man are gradually subjugated by higher responses through cultivation and education of the intellectual and spiritual capacities.

7.2 Human body

The human physical reality is fully manifested in the human body. This is a complex system consisting of many elements that collectively and coherently operate to support human life in the physical world. Every cell, every organ and every nerve plays a role in sustaining human life.

The human body is the link between human reality and the physical world. It is nourished from the resources provided in the material world, and as it grows from infancy to maturity, it manifests all the potentialities hidden in it. When physical life has ended, the body disintegrates and returns to the mineral world.

The intellectual and spiritual realities assist in bringing to fruition the powers of the human body. They also interact with the physical world through the human body. For example, the power of the intellectual reality of man is manifested as a result of the interaction between the human spirit and the human brain. The mind, which represents the human intellectual capacity, only works effectively when the human brain is sound enough.

7.3 Sensory perception

Sensory perception provides man with an awareness of his environment. This characteristic is held in common between human and animal in terms of its mechanism and operation.

A "sense" is a faculty through which the body perceives an external stimulus. It consists of a group of sensory cell types associated with a specific region within the brain where signals are received and processed. Based on this criterion, some studies have identified as many as twenty-one senses in human, many more than the five originally identified by Aristotle. However, bio-psychologists, still divide the senses into the five major groups: vision, hearing, touch, balance, and taste/smell. The receptor cells in each sensory organ convert the environmental stimuli into electrical nerve impulses that are carried by neurons to the brain for processing.

The process of sensory perception by the brain is instantaneous, effortless and, generally, accurate. For example, we can identify people by their face or voice. We can also judge how hot the water in the shower is or recognise a flower by its fragrance. Apart from individual likes and dislikes, our sensory perception usually agrees with the perception of other people. Therefore, what we perceive exists in the physical world and is not created in our mind.

Neurons are the nerve cells that form the central nervous system, which comprises the brain and spinal cord. There are several types of neuron, with specialised functions such as receiving and conducting electric impulses as well as processing and transmitting information to other organs. A neuron, as illustrated in Figure 7.1, consists of a cell body (2) the nucleus (3), a single axon (4) that sends messages by conveying electrical signals to other neurons, and a set of dendrites (1), which forms a synapse (junction gap) with the dendrites of another neuron across which the signals are transmitted by the diffusion of a chemical neurotransmitter.

The function of sensory perception is performed by a large proportion of the brain's cells, which are located in the cerebral cortex. Over half of the neurons in the cerebral cortex are used to process visual signals. The processes involved in perception are very complex and are not yet fully understood. Despite great advances in computer technology, we still have not been able to build a general-purpose computer that can perform even the lowest degrees of perception. The automatic diagnostic systems such as the ones used to detect abnormalities in medical images are quite limited in their scope and reliability. Human perception is illustrated in Figure 7.2.

Brain damage caused by accidents or disease can result in a dramatic malfunctioning of perception. For example, an individual may not be able to recognise his/her own face in the mirror.

7.4 Instinctive responses

Empirical evidence indicates that humans share common responses to certain stimuli from the time of their birth. For example, when an object touches an infant's mouth, it sucks automatically. Some of these innate responses, also known as "instinctive responses", gradually disappear as children grow, while others continue for the rest of their lives. Observations show that innate responses are universal among all human beings regardless of their culture, background or nationality. They are hard-coded in the DNA within the genes of the cells. Instincts exist in the physical reality of both man and animals.

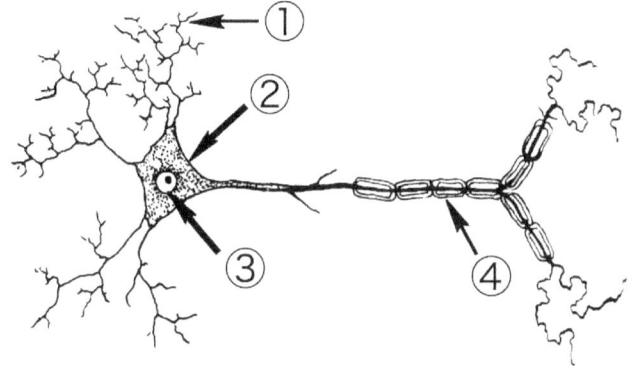

Figure 7.1 – Structure of a neuron

An instinct can be defined as a simple, direct, spontaneous and reactive response to a specific stimulus. Instincts are not the product of learning but are hard-wired within the genes, and hence organisms are born with them. For example, instinctive activities such as reproduction and food gathering in insects are not based on previous experience.

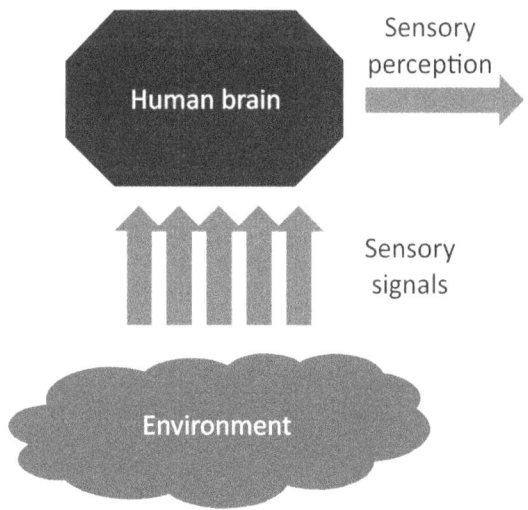

Figure 7.2 – Human sensory perception

Instincts usually trigger the organism to initiate a specific activity. This activity can be modified through experience. For example, nest building by birds is triggered by an instinct. The structure and shape of the nest are also predetermined, although they can be modified according to what materials are available in the environment.

Instincts are an integral part of human physical reality. They have developed during evolution as man was forced to adapt to his environment to survive. There are many classes of instincts identified in man such as food gathering and protective responses. For example, early man developed an instinct to hunt and kill for food as well as to protect himself from wild animals.

There are differences in the role and function of instincts between humans and animals. The behaviour of an animal is largely dictated by its instincts. However, many of man's instincts are gradually subjugated by other responses through cultivation and education of his intellectual and spiritual capacities. The powers of decision making and moral judgement can affect human responses to the extent that they oppose those dictated by instincts.

The instincts of animals, however, are dominant and permanent though responses can be adapted to new situations through learning at the individual level and through evolution at the species level.

7.5 Genes and instincts

As mentioned in the previous chapters, the basic structural unit of every complex organism is the cell, which contains inherited genetic information packaged in the form of genes. Every gene is composed of a length of DNA that has information encoded in its chemical structure. The genes provide the instructions that give organisms their particular characteristics—such as eye and hair colour that are passed on to the next generation.

Although the four basic chemical building blocks in DNA are the same for every living organism, the ordering or sequence of these building blocks varies from species to species, and less so from individual to individual of the same species. This variation is what determines an organism's physical characteristics and innate responses. Therefore, any alteration within the DNA structure, whether it be a change in the order of the chemical sequence, the removal of an existing sequence, the insertion of a new sequence, or by "turning on or off" certain genes, will result in some change in those characteristics. Genes, in their role of shaping our reflex responses, can be considered as the innate determinants of behaviour.

The genetic information contained in every cell of an organism is essentially the same (some variation occurs due to mutations). As each cell divides, the genes also divide and one set is transmitted to each new cell.

Empirical studies have shown that the DNA structure of the brain's neuron cells determines our instinctive responses.

7.6 Activities

7.6.1 Multiple choice questions

1. Sensory perception provides man with _____.
    A. an understanding of reality
    B. awareness of everything that is observable
    C. awareness of everything that is abstract
    D. all of the above

2. Sensory perception is _____.
    A. exclusive to man
    B. exclusive to animals
    C. common in both animals and man
    D. none of the above

3. The major senses include _____.
    A. vision and hearing
    B. touch and balance
    C. taste and smell
    D. all of the above

4. The stimuli received by sensors are converted to _____ and transferred to brain by _____.
    A. electrical nerve pulses; blood vessels
    B. mechanical nerve pulses; neurons
    C. electrical nerve pulses; neurons
    D. mechanical nerve pulses; blood vessels

5. Our perception of our environment _____ the perception of others.
    A. is closely similar to
    B. is often different from
    C. is never similar to
    D. is never different from

6. The dendrites in a neuron _____.
    A. transmit the signals to other neurons
    B. send a message by conveying electrical signals to other neurons
    C. are the nuclei of the neuron
    D. none of the above

7. The axon in a neuron _____.
    A. transmits the signals to other neurons
    B. sends message by conveying electrical signal to other neurons
    C. is the nucleus of the neuron
    D. none of the above

8. Instincts are _____.
    A. low level perceptions
    B. automatic responses to certain stimuli
    C. attitudes in an individual
    D. none of the above

9. Human instincts _____.
    A. gradually disappear as people grow
    B. stay with the individuals for the rest of their lives
    C. do not exist in some individuals
    D. none of the above

10. Human instincts _____.
    A. vary according to race and culture
    B. are universal among all, independent from race and culture
    C. vary according to ethnicity
    D. none of the above

11. Instincts exist _____.
    A. only in man
    B. only in animals
    C. in both man and animals
    D. none of the above

12. Instincts _____.
    A. are hard-wired in the genes
    B. are the product of learning
    C. do not exist at the time of birth
    D. none of the above

13. The genes _____.
    A. provide the instructions that give organisms their instincts.
    B. determine the physical characteristics of an organism
    C. both A and B
    D. none of the above

14. The information within the genes is encoded in the _____
    A. DNA
    B. neurons
    C. nervous system
    D. none of the above
15. The four basic elements of DNA _____.
    A. exist in every organism
    B. are the same in every organism
    C. have different sequences in every organism
    D. all of the above
16. Human and animal instincts are _____.
    A. identical
    B. very different
    C. have some similarities
    D. none of the above
17. Instincts usually trigger man to _____.
    A. feel in a particular way
    B. have a mood change
    C. act in a particular way
    D. none of the above

7.6.2 Short answer questions

1. What is meant by sensory perception?

   _____
   _____
   _____
   _____

2. How does sensory perception function?

   _____
   _____
   _____
   _____

3. What are the main differences between sensory perception in man and animals?

4. What are instincts?

5. What are the main differences between instincts in man and animals?

6. How are instincts acquired?

7. How are instincts transferred from one generation to another?

7.6.3 Projects
1. Design a poster to illustrate how your sensory perception works. Show an example in your poster.

2. Reflect on yourself and identify some of your behaviours that you think are based on instincts.

8 Human Intellectual Reality

8.1 Introduction

In this chapter human intellectual reality is explored. Through our intellectual reality we are able to think through issues and then make choices and decisions. The core element of intellectual reality is the human mind. This is a set of cognitive faculties that enables consciousness of self; awareness of the world and our experiences; logical thinking and extrapolation; making judgements, choices and plans; feeling emotions; and selectively storing and recalling memories. The mind is a non-tangible entity that cannot be directly associated with any part of the human body.

Over many centuries philosophers have tried to explore the nature of the mind in an attempt to understand it. However, neither the physical sciences nor psychology has been able to provide a conclusive explanation of the nature of the mind.

In this chapter, you need to reflect on and understand the following key points:

a) The human intellectual reality distinguishes man from other species.
b) The intellectual reality of man gives man the power to consciously utilise the information gleaned from his environment through his senses; and to think, understand and form judgments using logic and reasoning.
c) The core element of the intellectual reality is the mind.
d) Man's subjective consciousness and perception can develop abstract thoughts through two instruments: the human soul and the mind.

e) The human soul, through the power of inner vision, develops abstract thoughts without the assistance of the brain.
f) Although the mind and the power of inner vision work hand in hand, they cannot work simultaneously.
g) The mind emerges from the interaction of the mental powers of the soul, the power of reasoning, and the processing power of the human brain.

8.2 Nature of intellectual reality

While our physical reality is similar to that of animals, our ability to think through issues, to reflect on our experiences using our memory, and to change our actions and plans in light of our reflections, distinguish us significantly from all species of the animal kingdom. We have the ability to reflect on the choices available to us, to use reason to obtain the best option, and make a decision to implement the best choice. The power of reasoning is known as the human rational or intellectual reality and is unique to man. There is no evidence to indicate that animals have this faculty.

The power of reasoning is different from sensory perception. In sensory perception, the brain develops an understanding of the physical and tangible world through processing of the sensory information (consciousness and perception faculties). The intellectual reality of man uses the sensory information provided by his sensors and logic to think, understand and form judgments. This is known as the power of reasoning.

As mentioned in section 4.4 the power of reasoning is a power exclusive to man that is manifested when the human spirit acts upon the human brain. For example, if you arrive at a spot in a desert where trees and plants grow, you would conclude that somewhere there is water in that location without needing to see any water. This process of discovering unknown from known information is an example of the power of the intellectual perception of man.

8.3 Intellectual reality and the mind

The core element of intellectual reality is known as the mind. This is the faculty of consciousness and thought that enables us to use our perception to understand the world around and within us, to store our experiences in our memory, and to feel emotions and make judgements. The mind is a non-tangible entity that cannot be directly associated with any part of the human body. Many philosophers have been exploring the nature of the mind in an attempt to understand it. Some early philosophers such as Aristotle identified it as a part of the human soul.

Modern sciences started to emerge in the sixteenth and seventeenth centuries. This emergence influenced the early modern philosophers to identify a scientific worldview for their theories. Rene Descartes (31 March 1596—11 February 1650), the greatest philosophers of this period, suggested that the human mind and body were two distinctive and independent substances, whereas emotions were generated as the result of the interaction between the body and the mind.

During the eighteenth century, in the period known as the Enlightenment, philosophers developed a more materialistic view of the origin of man and the human mind. They proposed that the mind was the direct result of the activities of the human brain and physiological changes in the body. Recent scientific and medical discoveries indicate that thought processes are active in different parts of the brain. However, science does not understand how the powers of the mind emerge as a result of such activities. In other words, the physical sciences and psychology have not been able to provide a conclusive explanation for the nature of the mind.

8.4 Operation of intellectual reality

In the absence of a scientific explanation for the human intellectual reality and the mind, we have to draw on the model described in the Bahá'í Writings.[1] According to this model, man can use his perception to develop abstract thoughts through two instruments: the human soul (see section 9.3 for more details on the soul) and the mind.

The human soul, through its faculty of the power of inner vision, develops abstract thoughts without the assistance of the brain. In contrast, the human mind uses prior knowledge (the memory) and the power of reasoning to develop abstract thoughts.

The power of inner vision of the soul and the mind do not work simultaneously. The power of inner vision can perceive when the

---

[1] Refer to a compilation of Bahá'í Writings by Henry A. Weil, *Drops from the Ocean*, 1997.

mind is still and vice versa. The mind makes all of the rational decisions, whereas all original and creative thoughts are generated through the faculty of inner vision.

The mind and the power of inner vision work hand in hand. A creative idea generated by the power of inner vision is passed to the mind. Through the power of reasoning, the mind decides whether to totally, partly or not to deploy an idea. In a reverse process, the mind can observe and compile the available evidences regarding a particular issue. The power of inner vision integrates the information provided by the mind and develops a collective understanding and perception.

8.4.1 Nature and function of the mind

The mind emerges from the interaction of the mental powers of the soul, the human spirit and its main faculty, the power of reasoning and the processing power of the human brain as illustrated in Figure 8.2. The four mental powers of the soul are: imagination, thought, understanding and memory.

In previous chapters we have studied the human brain and the power of reasoning. The mental powers of the soul will be studied in more detail in section 9.4 .

'Abdu'l-Bahá provides a powerful analogy to define the relationship between the human soul, the mental powers of the soul and the mind. He states these powers are: *"... the essential requisites of the reality of man, even as the solar ray is the inherent property of the sun. The temple of man is like unto a mirror, his soul is as the sun, and his mental faculties even as the rays that emanate from that source of light. The ray may cease to fall upon the mirror, but it can in no wise be dissociated from the sun."*[1]

---

[1] 'Abdu'l-Bahá, *Bahá'í World Faith*, p. 346.

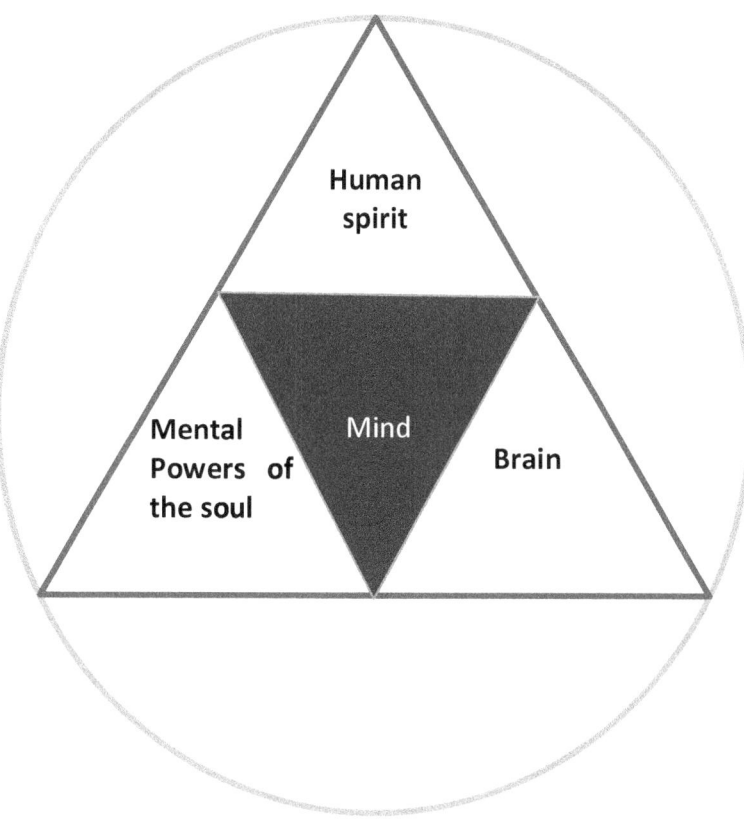

Figure 8.2 – Illustration of the formation of the Mind

8.5 Activities

8.5.1 Multiple choice questions

1. The intellectual reality of man provides the ability to _____.
   A. think
   B. reflect on experience
   C. make choices
   D. all of the above

2. Intellectual reality is _____.
   A. exclusive to man
   B. in common with animals
   C. different in animals
   D. none of the above

3. The power of reasoning _____.
   A. is the same as sensory perception
   B. utilizes sensory perception
   C. has common features with sensory perception
   D. all of the above

4. Through intellectual perception _____.
   A. man learns about his environment
   B. man processes sensory information
   C. the unknown can be derived from known information
   D. none of the above

5. The core element of intellectual reality is _____.
   A. the brain
   B. the mind
   C. the soul
   D. the power of reasoning

6. Aristotle believed that the mind was _____.
   A. the same as the brain
   B. the same as the soul
   C. was a substance independent and different from the physical body
   D. none of the above

7. Rene Descartes believed that the mind was _____.
   A. the same as the brain

B. the same as the soul
C. was a substance independent and different from the physical body
D. none of the above

8. During the period of Enlightenment, philosophers believed that the mind was _____.
   A. the same as the brain
   B. the same as the soul
   C. was a substance independent and different from the physical body
   D. none of the above

9. Man can develop abstract thoughts through _____.
   A. the mind
   B. the power of inner vision of the soul
   C. both the mind and the power of inner vision
   D. none of the above

10. The mind develops abstract thoughts through _____.
    A. sensory perception
    B. the power of reasoning
    C. the processing power of the brain
    D. none of the above

11. The power of inner vision and the mind _____.
    A. can work simultaneously
    B. do not work simultaneously
    C. have no interaction and association
    D. none of the above

12. The mind is responsible for _____.
    A. generating creative ideas
    B. generating feelings
    C. making decisions
    D. none of the above

13. The power of inner vision is responsible for _____.
    A. generating creative ideas
    B. generating feelings
    C. making decisions
    D. none of the above

14. The mind emerges _____.
    A. through the processing power of brain
    B. through the power of reasoning
    C. through the mental powers of the soul
    D. through all of the above
15. Among the mental powers of the soul are _____.
    A. imagination
    B. thought
    C. understanding
    D. all of the above
16. The mental powers of the soul _____.
    A. cannot make decisions on their own
    B. can make decisions on their own
    C. require the brain to make decisions
    D. none of the above

8.5.2 Short answer questions

1. What are the main characteristics of the human intellectual reality?

2. What is abstract thought?

3. How does man develop abstract thought?

4. How does the power of reasoning and sensory perception work together to develop abstract thoughts?
   _____
   _____
   _____
   _____

5. What is the power of inner vision?
   _____
   _____
   _____
   _____

6. What is the function of the power of inner vision?
   _____
   _____
   _____
   _____

7. What is the mind?
   _____
   _____
   _____
   _____

8. What is the function of the mind?
   _____
   _____
   _____
   _____

9. What is the difference between the mind and the power of inner vision?
   _____

10. Give an example of how the power of inner vision and the mind work together.

11. How is the human mind formed?

12. Give an analogy to describe the relationship between the human body, the soul and the mind.

8.5.3 Projects

1. Identify an occasion when you have used your power of inner vision. Illustrate the details in a poster.
2. Consider the following statement from 'Abdu'l-Bahá about the imagination:

    "... imagination is one of our greatest powers and a most difficult one to rule. Imagination is the father of superstition."[1]

---

[1] `Abdu'l-Bahá quoted in Grundy, *Ten Days in the Light of Akká*, p. 30.

Reflect on occasions that you have been affected by your imagination. Choose the one instance that has been misleading and a source of superstition. Design a poster to describe that imagined experience.

9 HUMAN SPIRITUAL REALITY

9.1 Introduction

Humans manifest characteristics that are fundamentally different from the characteristics and behaviour that originate from the physical and intellectual realities. The human spiritual reality has its roots in an entity known in philosophy and religion as the human soul. The spiritual reality of man and the nature of the soul will be studied in this chapter.

In this chapter, you need to reflect on and understand the following key points:

a) The manifestations of the spiritual reality of man are fundamentally different from the physical and intellectual realities.
b) In philosophy and religion, the origin of the human spiritual reality is known as the soul.
c) The soul of an individual comes into existence at the time of conception, when the first cell of the embryo is formed.
d) The human soul does not stem from the physical world and hence its nature is beyond our understanding.
e) The collective identity of an individual is represented by the soul.
f) The human soul is born with gifts and capacities to grow and transform.
g) The human soul can perceive and observe through the faculty of inner vision independent from the mind.
h) The moral choices we make affect our soul, and may advance or retard its growth.

9.2 Evidences of spiritual reality

Whenever we are able to observe people more closely, we can recognise qualities in them over and above physical characteristics such as their gender, skin-colour and age, as well as their intellectual capacities as expressed in their speech. Our perceptions of who they really are will tend to revolve around what we have discovered lies behind their thoughts, feelings and ideas.

As highlighted in chapter 6, man manifests characteristics that are fundamentally different from the characteristics realized through human physical and intellectual realities. For example, one of the instinctive behaviours originating from our physical reality is self-protection or self-care. However, we see some people are prepared to endanger themselves to help others or sacrifice their time, wealth and comfort in order to achieve some good for others and human society. The wholesome human feelings such as love, generosity, justice, kindness, and joy go beyond instinctive behaviour. These are all manifestations of another reality of man that we call spiritual reality.

9.3 Spiritual reality and the soul

Identification and understanding of human spiritual reality goes beyond the natural sciences, as its evidences and manifestations cannot be observed or measured by instruments developed for scientific observations and discoveries. Despite a great deal of effort, the humanities and social sciences have also failed to provide a unified and conclusive explanation of human spiritual reality.

As the physical reality of man originates from the body and the intellectual reality from the mind, human spiritual reality must have another source associated with man. In the social sciences, in particular psychology and psychiatry, the distinctive spiritual characteristics of man have been recognized and studied. However, such characteristics are assumed to be associated with the human mind.

In religion and philosophy, the origin of human spiritual reality is known as the soul. The word "soul" is a translation of the ancient Greek word "psyche", used in English words such as "psychology" and "psychiatry". In Latin, the word translated as soul is "anima", which is the root of words such as "animism", "animated" and "animator" in English.

Some philosophers such as Aristotle and Descartes suggested that the identity of an individual was represented by the soul. However, they also assumed that the soul was an inherent property of the human mind. While the human soul contributes to the functioning of the mind (as mentioned in chapter 8), the mind is fundamentally distinct from the soul.

9.4 Powers and functions of the soul

Our understanding of the human soul comes primarily from the teachings of various religions revealed to humanity over the last six thousand years. Nearly all major religions consider the spiritual reality of man as an important aspect of his development. In this chapter, we shall study the nature of the human soul based on the teachings of the Bahá'í Faith[1], which represents the latest guidance from God for the advancement of human material and spiritual civilization in this age.

According to these teachings, the soul of an individual originates at the time of conception, when the first cell of the embryo is formed.[2] Then, as with the physical body and the mind, the human soul commences its growth and development towards maturation and perfection.

The human soul is not from the physical world and hence its nature is beyond our understanding. Bahá'u'lláh, the Prophet Founder of the Bahá'í Faith, describes the human soul as "... *one of the signs of God, a mystery among His mysteries.*"[3] Since the soul is not made of matter, it is not governed by physical laws and is completely independent from the body. While the physical body is alive, the human soul is closely associated with the body and acts through it. On the death of the physical body, the human soul survives, and continues its development and progress for all eternity.

---

[1] Information on the Bahá'í Faith is available from www.bahai.org.
[2] Shoghi Effendi in *Lights of Guidance*, p. 504.
[3] Bahá'u'lláh, *Gleanings from the Writings of Bahá'u'lláh*, p. 160.

The human soul plays a crucial role in the life-experience of the body while the body is alive. The interactions of the soul with the physical body are described in the following sections.

9.4.1 Interaction with the physical world

The soul, a spiritual entity, interacts with the physical world through communication with the brain. The spiritual perception realized through the senses in the brain are passed to the soul. The soul in turn transmits its desires and intentions to different organs of the body via the brain. Hence, the soul can express itself through the tongue or perform a task through the actions of the hands.[1]

9.4.2 Identity of an individual

As highlighted in previous chapters, physiologically, we consist of many clusters of cells that perform different functions within the body. Each cell carries the biological identity of each individual in the form of genes within the DNA. The collective identity of an individual is represented by the soul. This identity reflects the status of the soul, the degree of its progress, and the extent of the development of the spiritual attributes inherent within the soul.

9.4.3 Capacity for growth and transformation

Similar to the physical body, the human soul is also born with latent gifts and capacities for spiritual growth and transformation. For example, our capacity to develop virtues such as love, generosity, kindness, justice and others are part of these hidden gifts. Through proper nurture and education of the soul, such capacities can be cultivated and unveiled during the lifetime of an individual.

9.4.4 Spiritual perception

The human soul provides an alternative method for perception through the faculty of inner vision. Through this power, one can perceive independently from the body. The human mind develops abstract thoughts by assimilating sensory information and evidences, whereas the soul develops both intuitive and abstract thoughts by itself, independently from the mind. The difference is that the faculty of inner vision knows, whereas the mind has to reason its way through issues.

---

[1] 'Abdu'l-Bahá, *Paris Talks*, p. 86.

Hence, the faculty of inner vision can be considered as a second source of human thought. It operates when the mind is not functioning. The mind makes all the decisions and choices; whereas all the intuitive, innovative and creative thoughts originate from the faculty of inner vision.

9.4.5 Reflecting virtuous choices

The moral choices that we make through our power of reasoning and decision making affect the progress of our soul. A virtuous decision or deed accelerates our spiritual growth. On the other hand, wrong or non-virtuous choices leave negative traces on our soul that can slow or halt our spiritual progress, and can cause spiritual unhappiness. For example, when we lie or engage in backbiting, our soul is adversely affected. In addition, like an adding machine, the soul registers the sum total of all the virtuous and non-virtuous choices that we make during our physical lifetime.

Hence, our soul is like a hinged mirror that we can tilt it up towards loftiness and happiness, or down towards abasement and lowliness through the choices we make.

9.4.6 Assisting mental processes of the mind

The mental processes in man are quite complex. They are produced as the result of the interaction between the spiritual powers of the soul and the processing power of the human brain. The human intellectual power cannot manifest itself without the power of the soul. This was explained in more detail in section 8.4.1.

The soul emanates four mental powers: imagination, thought, comprehension and memory. These powers, are called inward powers in contrast to the physical senses that are known as outward powers. The inward powers, though essential in the process of human decision making, cannot make a decision on their own until they are acted upon by the power of reasoning and assisted by the brain.

Imagination is the power of creating images and pictures in the mind without outwardly observing them. Thought is the process of forming an idea, opinion, plan, etc. in the mind and is an intrinsic characteristic of man, reflecting his reality. Comprehension is the ability to understand the reality of things. Through the power of memory, man stores and recalls what is imagined, thought and understood.[1]

For example, an image perceived by the human sight is passed to the inner powers through the common faculty. The power of imagination conceives and forms that image and transmits it to the power of thought. The power of though grasps the reality of the image by reflecting on it and conveys it to the power of comprehension. After understanding the image, it is passed to the memory and kept in its repository.

The interaction between the mental powers of the soul and the brain is illustrated in Figure 9.1.

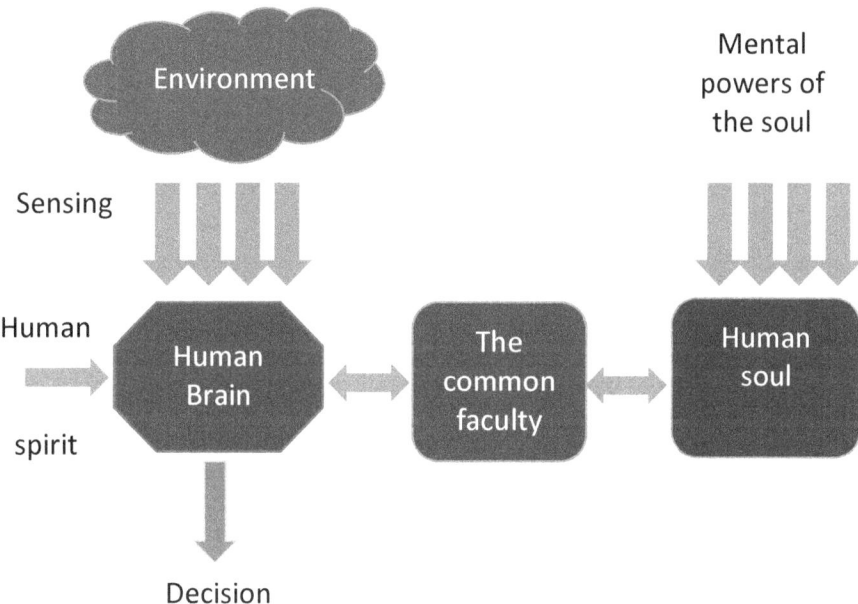

Figure 9.1 – Interaction between the soul and the brain

---

[1] 'Abdu'l-Bahá, *Some Answered Questions*, p. 210.

9.5 Activities

9.5.1 Multiple choice questions

1. The word "soul" is a translation of the word _____.
    A. psyche in Greek
    B. anima in Latin
    C. both A and B
    D. none of the above

2. The human soul _____.
    A. is part of the mind
    B. is independent from the mind
    C. is an illusion of the mind
    D. none of the above

3. The spiritual reality of man originates from the _____.
    A. the physical body and the brain
    B. the mind
    C. the soul
    D. none of the above

4. The human soul is created _____.
    A. at the time of conception
    B. when the baby is born
    C. when the individual reaches maturity
    D. None of the above

5. The human soul _____.
    A. is governed by physical laws
    B. is not governed by physical laws
    C. is governed by some of physical laws
    D. none of the above

6. The collective identity of an individual is represented by _____.
    A. the brain
    B. the mind
    C. the soul
    D. none of the above

7. Rene Descartes believed that the mind was _____.
    A. the same as brain

B. the same as soul
C. a substance independent and different from the physical body
D. none of the above

8. The human soul grows _____.
   A. through our efforts by developing its inner gifts
   B. naturally as the physical body grows
   C. through effective intellectual education
   D. none of the above

9. Spiritual perception is _____.
   A. intellectual perception assisted by the soul
   B. the discovery of the soul independent from the mind
   C. the experience of imagination
   D. None of the above

10. The power of inner vision is the source of _____.
    A. intuition
    B. innovations
    C. creativity
    D. all of the above

11. Moral choices are _____.
    A. the decisions we make about our future
    B. the decisions we make based on our likes and dislikes
    C. the decisions we make based on our behaviour towards others
    D. all of the above

12. Which of the following is not a virtuous choice?
    A. being cruel to someone
    B. lying
    C. being selfish
    D. All of the above

13. The power of inner vision is responsible for _____.
    A. generating creative ideas
    B. generating feelings
    C. making decisions
    D. none of the above

14. The progress of the soul is affected by our_____.

    A. virtuous choices
    B. choices that are not virtuous
    C. both A and B
    D. none of the above
15. Like a hinged mirror, the soul _____.
    A. reflects what our thoughts focus on
    B. can be used to explore the world spiritually
    C. assists our power of imagination
    D. all of the above

9.5.2 Short answer questions

1. What indicates that man has another reality besides the physical and intellectual realities?

   _____
   _____
   _____
   _____

2. What is the source of the human spiritual reality?

   _____
   _____
   _____
   _____

3. Compare the creation of the soul and its growth with the birth and growth of the physical body.

   _____
   _____
   _____
   _____

4. Why is the soul not governed by physical laws?

   _____
   _____

5. What is the identity of an individual?

6. What is the capacity of the soul for growth and transformation?

7. What are the differences between the spiritual perception of the soul and the intellectual perception of the mind?

8. How do our moral choices affect the progress of our soul?

9. What are the mental powers of the soul? Describe each one of them.

_____
_____
_____

9.5.3 Projects

1. Reflect on yourself. Can you identify the evidences of your soul within yourself?
2. Reflect on the moral choices that you have made in the past. Identify which ones have been virtuous and which ones non-virtuous? Explain your reasons for each category.

10 Self

10.1 Introduction

In this chapter we explore the concept of the self. Over the last three thousand years, many philosophers have tried to understand and explain the self. Amongst their reflections, the self was studied in the context of religion as a means of understanding the evils of egotism, selfishness and self-centredness; and its harmful consequences to the behaviour of individuals and to the health of the community. In recent decades, psychologists and social scientists have finally accepted that the self is the key to understanding human behaviour. Despite intensive research, no universally accepted single concept and definition of the self has emerged. We will study the nature of the self in the following sections.

In this chapter, you need to reflect on and understand the following key points:

a) The concept of the self has been studied by many philosophers over the past three thousand years.
b) Philosophers have been reflecting on the self, based on religious teachings that enhance one's spirituality.
c) In recent decades psychologist and social scientists have accepted that the self is the key to understanding human behaviour.
d) Despite intensive research in psychology and social sciences, no universally accepted single concept and definition of the self has emerged.
e) In philosophy and religion, the concept of the self has been used in different contexts: in association with our individuality and in reference to our lower nature.

f) The influence of the physical, intellectual and spiritual realities on the self can be modelled respectively as "physical-self", "intellectual-self" and the "spiritual-self".

10.2 In Search of the self

The concept of the self has been the focal point of study of many philosophers over the past three thousand years. Eastern philosophers have been reflecting on the self based on religious teachings that enhance one's spirituality. For example, the *Upanishads*, which was written in India as early as 600 BC, the *Tao Te Ching* in China around 500 BC and the teachings of Gautama Buddha from around 563–483 BC have dealt deeply and extensively with questions about the self and identity. Plato was the first philosopher known to use an intellectual approach to study the self, circa 428–347 BC.

Many of the findings and insights of the early philosophers were accurate and perceptive, and have been confirmed by empirical studies conducted by present day behavioural and social scientists.

For nearly the next two thousand years after those earliest reflections, the concept of self was mainly analysed in the context of religion as a means of understanding the evils of egotism, selfishness and self-centredness; and its harmful effects on the behaviour of individuals and the spiritual and social health of the community. The aim was to identify methods by which an individual could overcome those ego-driven negative attitudes and behaviours that hamper spiritual development.

During the Enlightenment, most of the great philosophers, such as Descartes, Locke, Hume, Leibnitz, Berkeley, and Kant, continued to search for an understanding of the self. William James (January 11, 1842—August 26, 1910) was the first scientist to develop a detailed psychological discussion of the self in his book *The Consciousness of Self*. However, for many decades after this seminal publication, psychologists remained hesitant to engage with such invisible internal concepts as the self, and avoided the line of investigation that James had followed.

In recent decades psychologists and social scientists have finally accepted that knowledge of the self is the key to understanding human behaviour. In such studies, the term "self" has been used in many different contexts—these can be grouped into five categories:[1]

a) Self as the total person commonly used in everyday language.
b) Self referring to all or part of an individual's personality. This implies that the self is a collection of abilities, values, preferences, attitudes and aspirations.
c) Self as an entity in the individual that experiences life and registers those experiences.
d) Self referring to perceptions, thoughts and feelings about oneself, and providing answers to questions such as "Who am I?" and "What am I?"
e) Self as a decision maker, a doer, and an agent that regulates people's behaviour.

In spite of intensive research in psychology and the social sciences, no universally accepted concept and definition of "self" has emerged.

10.3 Self in religion and philosophy

In philosophy and religion, the word "self" has been used in different contexts. In one context, "self" is associated with our individuality. For every one of us, the human reality assumes and manifests unique qualities and characteristics that collectively form our unique identity. This is known as "the self". The self cannot be located anywhere inside our body and cannot be touched. However, we are aware of it and it has a presence that we can feel. Hence, the self is metaphysical and nonmaterial.

In another context, "self" refers to our lower nature, which is a representation of our physical reality. The manifestation of our lower nature in our deeds and words and observed by others is usually known as the ego. The ego represents the self that is the protector and defender of our internal impulses, and is the heritage of our material origin. The ego can become a source of selfishness and brutality if it is not controlled and subdued.

The noble and heavenly aspects of an individual are known as "the higher self". In order to subdue the lower self and the ego, the higher self should be strengthened. In religious teachings, the process of

---

[1] Mark, R. Leary, June P. Tangney, "The self as an organising construct in behavioural and social sciences", in *Handbook of Self and Identity*, ed. Mark, R. Leary, June P. Tangney, p. 8, The Guildford Press, 2003.

subordinating the ego and its desires to the noble characteristics of the higher self is referred to as "self-sacrifice".

10.4 Modelling self, based on human reality

Some reflections on the definitions given so far for the self in the previous sections indicate that they reflect the influence of different aspects of our reality on our identity. In order to develop a mental model of the self, the relationship between our physical, intellectual and spiritual realities, and different aspects of the self will be explored.

The lower self can represent the influence of physical reality on the identity of an individual. On the other hand, the higher-self can be considered as reflecting the authority of the spiritual-reality on the self. The definitions of "self", given in (d) and (e) of section 10.2 may be considered as the impact of the intellectual reality on the self. Based on this model, we define the influences of the physical, intellectual and spiritual realities on the self respectively as "physical-self", "intellectual-self" and the "spiritual-self". Hence, the behaviour of the self can be the result of the interaction and cooperation between the "physical-self", the "intellectual-self" and the "spiritual-self", (Figure 10.1). Such definitions are just constructs and represent only one possible model of the self.

Based on the analysis so far, we make the following formal definitions:

- The **physical-self** represents our animal side based on instinctual behaviour and our material origin.
- The **spiritual-self** is our higher self and represents the supernal qualities and attributes that we have developed within us. We are born with these qualities as potentialities in our souls. Such gifts become embedded qualities within us as a result of our efforts to cultivate and develop them.
- The **intellectual-self** is related to our intellectual abilities, such as identifying the truth and making decisions. In reaching a decision, our intellectual-self is affected by both our physical-self and spiritual-self. The quality and nature of the decision will depend on the capabilities of our intellectual-self, as well as the degree of influence exerted by the physical-self and spiritual-self. We will explore the dynamic of decision making in future chapters.

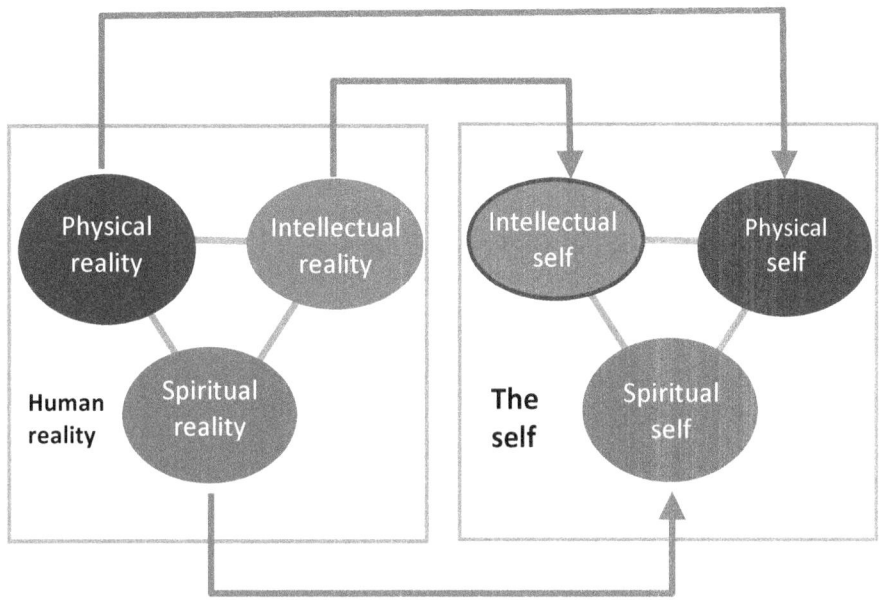

Figure 10.1 – Relationship between the human reality and the self

10.5 Activities

10.5.1 Multiple choice questions

1. The study of the self _____.
    - A. goes back thousands of years
    - B. started during the Enlightenment
    - C. started a few decades ago
    - D. none of the above

2. Early studies of the self were focused on _____.
    - A. enhancing people's spirituality
    - B. the evils of egotism
    - C. questions about the self and identity
    - D. all of the above

3. The first philosopher to take an intellectual approach to the study of the self was _____.
    - A. Gautama Buddha
    - B. Plato
    - C. Descartes
    - D. Kant

4. The first scientist to develop a detailed discussion of the self was _____.
    - A. Descartes
    - B. Hume
    - C. Kant
    - D. James

5. The collective identity of an individual is represented by _____.
    - A. the brain
    - B. the mind
    - C. the soul
    - D. none of the above

6. In the early 20th century, psychologists were hesitant to study the self because it was _____.
    - A. in the domain of philosophy
    - B. in the domain of religion
    - C. an invisible internal concept

D. all of the above
7. Understanding the self is the key to understanding _____.
   A. the mind
   B. the soul
   C. human behaviour
   D. all of the above
8. In philosophy and religion, the self represents _____.
   A. our ego
   B. the lower self
   C. both A and B
   D. none of the above
9. The physical-self is a manifestation of our _____.
   A. physical reality
   B. intellectual reality
   C. spiritual reality
   D. all of the above
10. The intellectual-self is a manifestation of our _____.
    A. physical reality
    B. intellectual reality
    C. spiritual reality
    D. all of the above
11. The spiritual-self is a manifestation of our _____.
    A. physical reality
    B. intellectual reality
    C. spiritual reality
    D. all of the above
12. The spiritual-self represents our _____.
    A. instinctual behaviour
    B. our supernal qualities and attributes
    C. intellectual abilities
    D. none of the above
13. The intellectual self represents our _____.
    A. instinctual behaviour
    B. our supernal qualities and attributes
    C. intellectual abilities
    D. None of the above

14. The physical self represents our _____.
    A. instinctual behaviour
    B. our supernal qualities and attributes
    C. intellectual abilities
    D. none of the above

10.5.2 Short answer questions

1. Who were the first people to study the concept of the self?

   _____

2. What was the focus of early studies on the self?

   _____

3. Why have religion and philosophy been interested in the concept of the self?

   _____

4. Why were the early psychologists not interested in the study of the self?

   _____

5. Who was the first psychologist to address the concept of the self in his work?

_____
_____
_____
_____

6. What are the five categories of the self, which are used by modern psychologists and social scientists?

_____
_____
_____
_____

7. In what contexts has the term "self" been used in philosophy and religion?

_____
_____
_____
_____

8. What is the ego?

_____
_____
_____
_____

9. What is the relationship between our reality and the self?

_____
_____
_____
_____

10. Describe your understanding of the following:

   a) Physical-self

   _____

   _____

   b) Intellectual-self

   _____

   _____

   c) Spiritual-self

   _____

   _____

11. How do the physical and spiritual selves affect the decision of the intellectual-self?

   _____

   _____

   _____

   _____

10.5.3 Projects

1. Reflect on yourself. Can you identify some of the characteristics of your physical-self, intellectual self and spiritual self? List them in bullet form for each category.
2. Consider a major moral decision you have recently made. Can you identify the role of your physical-self and spiritual-self in reaching this decision?

11 Ego

11.1 Introduction

The ego can be defined as that aspect of the self that is manifested in our words and deeds and observed by others. The characteristics and behaviour of the ego is determined by the degree of influence exerted on it by the spiritual-self and the physical-self. The dynamics of this behaviour can be considered as a spectrum that at one end is the self-centred noisy ego, which forcefully states its unique views and values, and imposes them on others. In this condition the ego is strongly influenced by the physical-self. At the other end is the very quiet ego that is under the influence of the spiritual-self. In this condition, the ego is completely detached from the self and transcends self-interest and the desire to dominate others. We explore the nature of the ego in this chapter.

In this chapter, you need to reflect on and understand the following key points:

a) The ego is that aspect of the self that can be observed by others through our behaviour.
b) The ego develops a tendency to protect the self, and often attempts to dominate and control others when it is under the influence of the physical-self.
c) The ego under the influence of the physical-self is known as the noisy ego.
d) The ego under the influence of the spiritual self transcends self-interest.
e) The ego influenced by the spiritual-self is known as the quiet ego.

f) Every individual is usually on a journey of spiritual growth from a very noisy ego towards a very quiet ego.

11.2 Definition of the ego

The ego can be defined as that aspect of the self that is manifested in our words and deeds, and observed by others. It represents the self that is the protector and defender of our internal impulses. The existence of the ego can be inferred from the behaviour of an individual but it cannot be directly observed.

The way we perceive the ego can be compared to how we perceive electricity. We cannot see electricity but we can understand it and get an idea of its strength by observing some of its effects. Another analogy is the power generated by a car engine. We cannot explicitly observe the power, but we can see the effect of it through the motion it produces in the car.

In a similar way, we can observe the ego by assessing certain behavioural characteristics in the individual. We can also determine to what extent the physical and spiritual selves have influenced the ego.

Although animals have the same physical reality as man, they have no consciousness about themselves and consequently no physical self as such. The behaviour of animals is mainly driven by their instincts. Also, since animals do not have intellectual and spiritual realities, they do not have the spiritual and intellectual selves. Animals, therefore, lack any ego equivalent to what exists in humans.

11.3 Influence of the physical-self on the ego

As mentioned in the previous chapters, the physical self is driven by instincts, one of which is to protect and advance the self. The effect of such tendencies on the ego is the emergence of certain behaviours tending to dominate and control others. An ego under the strong influence of the physical self is known as the noisy ego. A noisy ego shows extreme self-interest, has excessive greed for power and control, and demands attention.

Self-interest means giving priority and prominence to the self in thought, attitude and deeds. This results in selfishness, self-centredness and excessive self-love. A selfish ego places a person's own needs or desires above the needs or desires of others.

Paradoxically, studies conducted by psychologists indicate that self-interest is ultimately not in our own interest, and its harm goes beyond social disharmony. Self-interest often results in disunity, conflict and cruelty. There are many examples in human history of people under the influence of an extremely noisy ego causing severe oppression and cruelty. Although self-interest might bring some short-term gains, in the long term, it adversely affects the health and wellbeing of the individual.

The dominating, competitive culture of present day society encourages and supports the self-centred behaviour of the ego. For example, people are encouraged to acquire the largest, the biggest and the best, and to be first. In particular the struggle to be first tends to undermine unity and fellowship, and often results in separateness. Envy, jealously and covetousness are some of the harmful by-products of our competitive society.

The noisy ego works towards achieving its objectives through direct or indirect methods. Direct methods are obvious and active, and include using physical force, bullying and boasting.

However, the noisy ego seldom makes use of these direct methods to achieve its own way. It usually uses less obvious methods, which can be so subtle that we often do not recognize that certain acts are expressions of self-love and excessive noisiness. Examples of indirect methods are:

- **Sulking**: In this condition, the noisy ego remains silent and resentful to gain the sympathy and support of others.
- **Whining**: The noisy ego complains or protests in a childish manner, often about trivial things.
- **Talking too much**: The noisy ego monopolises conversation in order to dominate others and to control a group discussion.
- **Demanding special privileges**: The noisy ego feels superior to others and expects special privileges in every situation.

It is important to distinguish between striving for excellence and being competitive. When one makes an effort to achieve excellence in an endeavour, the aim is to realize one's potential rather than to compete with others. The former is a meritorious and praiseworthy act.

11.4 Influence of the spiritual-self on the ego

The spiritual-self has the primary task of encouraging and empowering the ego to transcend self-interest. The effect of the spiritual-self on the ego depends on how well the inner capacities of the soul are cultivated and developed. A well-developed spiritual-self can subjugate a noisy ego and quieten it.

The impact of the spiritual-self on the ego can be very significant. In particular, as a result of the influence of the spiritual-self, a quiet ego can manifest the following five major attributes from which other qualities can develop:

- **Detachment:** A quiet ego has a strong self-awareness without being attached to the self. Hence, it does not need to make any effort to constantly defend the worth of the self.
- **Unity:** A quiet ego is able to relate to the views of other people and see matters from their perspectives. It has the ability to go beyond apparent differences and to develop unity and harmony with others.
- **Compassion**: A quiet ego approaches the self and others with acceptance, empathy and a desire for the well-being of all.
- **Humility**: A quiet ego has a deep sense of humility and an accurate knowledge of its abilities. It acknowledges its mistakes, imperfections and limitations, is open to new ideas and advice, and has the ability to forget the self and to connect with others. Humble people have good social relationships. Since they have no ambition to dominate others, they are willing to learn from others.
- **Spiritual growth**: A quiet ego is interested in the development of the qualities embedded in the spiritual self rather than in an immediate gratification of desires dictated by the physical self. This is the process of spiritual growth.

11.5 Journey of the ego

Our study of the ego in this chapter so far indicates that the behaviour of the ego is determined by how much it is influenced by the spiritual-self and the physical-self. The dynamics of this behaviour can be considered as a spectrum that, at one end, is the self-centred noisy ego, which forcefully states its unique views and values, and imposes them on others. In this condition the ego is strongly influenced by the physical-self. At the other end is the very quiet ego that is under the influence of the spiritual-self. In this condition the ego is completely detached from the self and transcends self-interest and the desire to dominate others. The very quiet ego reflects the mature stages of spiritual growth. Every individual is usually on a journey of spiritual growth from a very noisy ego towards a very quiet ego, as illustrated in Figure 11.1.

It is not possible to completely extinguish the ego as it is the identity associated with the physical reality of man. The ego exists as long as we are alive in this physical world. However, it is possible to control the ego. In a religious context, those who have achieved the highest degree of domination over their ego are known as "saints".

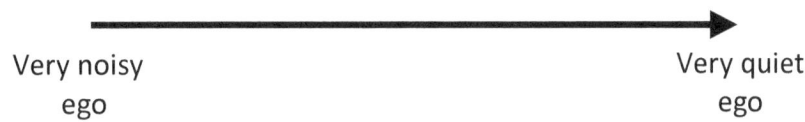

Very noisy ego   Very quiet ego

Figure 11.1 – Journey of the ego

11.6 Activities

11.6.1 Double choice questions

1. Indicate whether each statement is false or true.

		False	True
a)	The ego represents the physical-self.	☐	☐
b)	The ego is the behaviour of the self as observed by others.	☐	☐
c)	Animals have a physical reality. Hence, they have an ego.	☐	☐
d)	Animals have a physical reality. Hence, they have a physical self and an ego.	☐	☐
e)	Animals have a physical reality. However, they do not have consciousness about the self and they have no ego.	☐	☐
f)	The physical-self seeks superiority over others.	☐	☐
g)	An ego under the strong influence of the spiritual-self is known as a noisy ego.	☐	☐
h)	A noisy ego transcends self-interest.	☐	☐
i)	Self-interest means giving priority and prominence to the self in thought, attitude and deeds.	☐	☐
j)	A noisy ego always tries to achieve its objectives through direct methods.	☐	☐
k)	The main harm of self-interest is social disharmony.	☐	☐
l)	When sulking, a noisy ego remains silent and resentful to gain sympathy and the support of others.	☐	☐
m)	When whining, a noisy ego complains or protests in a childish manner, often about trivial things.	☐	☐
n)	The effect of the spiritual-self on the ego depends on how weak the physical-self is.	☐	☐

o) A quiet ego does not need to constantly defend the worth of the self. ☐ ☐

p) The impact of the spiritual-self on the ego can be quite significant and can transform the attitude and behaviour of the ego. ☐ ☐

2. In the following table, various behaviours of the ego are mentioned. For each behaviour, determine whether it is due to the influence of the physical-self (P-S) or the spiritual-self (S-S).

Behaviour of the ego	P-S	S-S
a) Transcends self-interest.	☐	☐
b) Protects and defends the self.	☐	☐
c) Dominates and controls others.	☐	☐
d) Has compassion for others.	☐	☐
e) Is humble.	☐	☐
f) Has greed for power and control.	☐	☐
g) Boasts about its successes.	☐	☐
h) Is detached from the self.	☐	☐
i) Demands attention.	☐	☐
j) Is interested in the development of hidden qualities.	☐	☐
k) Is interested in gratification of carnal desires.	☐	☐
l) Complains or protests in a childish manner.	☐	☐
m) Does not defend the worth of the self.	☐	☐
n) Relates to the views of other people.	☐	☐
o) Tends to monopolise conversation in order to dominate others.	☐	☐

11.6.2 Short answer questions

1. What is the ego?
_____
_____

2. Describe an analogy to illustrate the concept of the ego.
_____
_____
_____

3. Briefly describe the influence of the physical self on the ego.
_____
_____
_____

4. Briefly describe the influence of the spiritual self on the ego.
_____
_____
_____

5. What are the direct methods used by the ego to achieve its objectives?
_____

6. What are the indirect methods used by the ego to achieve its objectives?
_____
_____
_____

7. What are the five major qualities that a quiet ago can acquire under the influence of the spiritual self?
_____
_____
_____
_____

8. How can the ego be transformed from a noisy ego to a quiet ego?
_____
_____
_____

_____
_____

11.7 Project

Reflect on the following statements in connection with your ego. For each statement, answer the following questions:

    a) To what extent are they true for your ego?
    b) Would you like to strengthen or moderate them?
    c) What strategy are you going to use? Mention at least one?

Statements:

- Do I frequently find fault with others?
- Do I engage in backbiting?
- Do I listen to backbiting?
- Do I talk too much?
- Do I talk too little?
- Do I speak with too loud a voice?
- Do I speak with too soft a voice?
- Am I argumentative and quarrelsome when presenting my ideas?
- Do I use sarcasm and hurt the feelings of others with my cutting remarks?
- Do I whine and complain?
- Do I sulk? Do I "hold aloof" in a sullenly ill-humoured or offended manner?
- Do I give too much expression to my feelings of discouragement, depression or sadness, and thus darken the lives of others?
- Am I habitually late for appointments?
- Do I break my promises?
- Am I frequently indecisive?
- Do I make a boastful display of my intelligence, my attainments or my possessions?
- Do I show contempt for the feelings, ideas, or actions of others?
- Do I demand special privileges that deprive others of theirs?
- Do I dislike another person because he has a character trait like of my own, which I am trying to ignore in myself?

12 Inner Gifts and Capacities

12.1 Introduction

We are all born with gifts and capacities within our physical, intellectual and spiritual realities. These capacities are like a seed that will produce a mature tree and fruit when it receives care and nourishment. The nature of these inner gifts and capacities within every human being will be studied in this chapter.

In this chapter, you need to reflect on and understand the following key points:

a) Our first cell formed at the time of conception carries our complete physical characteristics and potentialities.
b) Our intellectual capacity can be considered as the potential inherent in our brain, our soul and our power of reasoning.
c) Our spiritual capacity for growth and transformation enables us to develop qualities and virtues.
d) Acquiring virtues and practising them requires the involvement of our soul, mind and the physical body.
e) Virtues are acquired through three interrelated stages of moral knowing, moral feeling and moral behaviour.

12.2 Capacities within

We are all born with gifts and capacities embedded within our reality. This is similar to the potentialities hidden in the seed of a tree. When the seed is planted, watered and looked after, the tree sprouts forth as a tender shoot and, as it grows, all the potentialities destined for it within the original seed are revealed in the form of branches, leaves, blossoms and fruits.

Bahá'u'lláh describes the capacities within the reality of an individual as the priceless gems hidden in a mine: *"Regard man as a mine rich in gems of inestimable value. Education can, alone, cause it to reveal its treasures, and enable mankind to benefit therefrom."*[1] The ground that holds within it the most precious gems such as diamonds may not appear different from any other terrain. The treasures that the ground hides are revealed when efforts are made to sift the sand or break up the rock and, thus, extract the gems. According to Bahá'u'lláh, education can bring forth the gifts hidden within the reality of man to the benefit of all.

All three aspects of our reality, physical, intellectual and spiritual, are endowed with these capacities, as will be studied in the following sections.

12.3 Physical capacities

Our first cell formed at the time of conception contains our complete physical characteristics and potentialities. On the first day after fertilisation, that cell started to divide and the process of building our various organs—such as our heart, brain and kidneys—gradually got underway through the differentiation and migration of our multiplying cells.

During the nine months' development of the embryo in the womb, the nourishment received through the mother's blood is crucial in producing healthy and well-functioning organs. At the time of birth, all the body's organs are physically developed but the growth of the physical body towards a complete, mature human being will continue for many years. Proper nourishment and thorough care of the body will ensure full realization of our potentialities and the capacities embodied in our genetic fingerprint.

The extreme performance demonstrated by athletes clearly shows that the ultimate human physical capacities are beyond what an average person will achieve. Expression of the genetic potential depends on the intensity, duration and frequency of the applied training, diet and other factors.

As we discussed in chapter 8, the intellectual reality of man emerges as the result of the interface and cooperation between the

---

[1] Bahá'u'lláh, *Gleanings from the Writings of Bahá'u'lláh*, p. 260.

brain, the power of reasoning and the soul. Hence, proper development of the brain is critical for the realization of human intellectual capacities.

12.4 Intellectual capacities

The potential intellectual ability of an individual is known as his/her intellectual capacities. As discussed in previous chapters, the core element of the intellectual reality is the mind. The mind emerges through the interaction of the mental powers of the soul, the human spirit and its power of reasoning, and the processing power of the human brain. Hence, the intellectual capacity can be considered as the potentials inherent in the brain and the soul. Human intellectual abilities, particularly the power of reasoning, emerges when the human spirit acts upon the intellectual capacities cultivated in the soul and the brain.

The brain consists of two types of cells: nerve cells, known as neurons, and glial cells. The number of neurons is about 100 billion and that of glial cells is about 10 to 50 times more. Glial cells play an important role in the brain—such as insulating neurons from each other. The brain cannot function effectively without glial cells.

The physical development of the brain starts at the time of conception and grows at a very rapid pace during its early stages. At some stage during embryonic development, as many as 250,000 neurons are added to the brain every minute. At the time of birth, the brain has nearly acquired all the neurons it requires. It then continues to grow for a few years after birth by increasing the number of its glial cells. Some recent studies also indicate that, in childhood, we develop new connections between groups of neurons called neural circuits.

After birth, the brain continues to grow and acquires a stronger mental capacity by interacting with the world through the body's sensory perceptions and actions. Information received from the body's sensors is transmitted through neurons as electrical signals. The information is further processed as it crosses the synapse between one neuron and another in the form of chemical signals.

The inner cognitive capacities of the mind are not evident at the time of birth but gradually unfold as the baby grows towards childhood, adolescence and adulthood. The ability for abstract thought and logical reasoning starts to mature around the age of 15.

12.5 Spiritual capacities

Similarly to the development of the physical body and the mind, the soul that represents the human spiritual reality is also born with many potentialities and hidden gifts. In chapter 9, we explored various powers and functions of the soul. One of them, the capacity for growth and transformation, plays a critical role in the development of our spiritual reality as it enables us to develop the positive qualities and attributes known as virtues.

Virtues such as love, generosity, kindness and justice are known as the foundation of a moral life; and represent moral excellence in an individual. They significantly affect our quality of life and happiness. Virtues are potentially embedded in the soul as hidden treasures.

Exploring the meaning of virtues and seeking a virtuous life date back to Socrates and to the work of his most famous student, Plato. Socrates and Plato studied the four virtues of prudence (discretion), justice, fortitude and courage, referred to as natural virtues. Later Aristotle provided a more systematic definition of virtue as "the state of character which makes a man good and which makes him do his own work well."[1]

Virtues have been a common thread among the teachings of all religions and traditions of all cultures of the world. In all the sacred literature and oral traditions of indigenous people, virtues and values are emphasised. Virtues are standards for ethical, moral and right conduct. Personal virtues, such as humility, gratitude and hope reflect a higher state of being.

12.6 Cultivating inner capacities

Developing and cultivating the physical, intellectual and spiritual capacities is a major responsibility of every individual during physical life. This includes:

a) Respecting the body, nurturing it, and ensuring its well-being.
b) Developing intellectual and aesthetic capacities through formal and systematic education.
c) Cultivating moral and spiritual capacities and insights.

Scientific and technological developments over the last two centuries have provided humanity with a deep understanding of how

---

[1] Howard J. Curzer, *Aristotle and the Virtues*, Oxford University Press, 2012, p. 52.

to cultivate human physical and intellectual capacities. We have a good understanding of how the human body works and how to nourish it through a proper diet and exercise. Schools and universities provide an effective environment for intellectual education of all ages, and for the development of human resources required for further advancement of material civilization.

In contrast, despite the complexity of human spiritual reality, cultivating spiritual capacities has received little attention in modern society. Further, it is neither appropriate nor adequate to apply methods developed for cultivating intellectual capacities to the development of spiritual capacities.

For example, "moral knowledge", i.e. learning about virtues and developing an understanding of them, does not lead to an embedding of the virtues within our character. An important step after moral knowledge is to develop a desire and attraction towards possessing the virtues. This is known as "moral feeling". The final step is to endeavour to embed these virtues in our character and to practice them in our attitude, words and deeds, leading to "moral behaviour".

The three stages of acquiring virtues; i.e. moral knowledge, moral feeling and moral behaviour; are associated with the three realities of man: intellectual reality, spiritual reality and physical reality. Hence, acquiring virtues requires an interaction and cooperation of our three realities through the mind, the soul and the body. Such relationships are illustrated in Figure 12.1.

Let us apply these concepts to the virtue of "compassion", which is a deep awareness of the suffering of another person with a desire to relieve it. We will not become compassionate just by learning about "compassion" (moral knowledge). We need to develop a deep attraction towards this virtue, become emotionally committed to it, and acquire a compassion to practice it. We should feel disturbed and uncomfortable when we behave without compassion, and feel outraged when we come across victims of suffering, exploitation or greed.

However, moral knowledge and having moral feelings do not make us compassionate. We must behave with compassion by acting compassionately in our personal relationships and fulfilling our obligations as citizens to help building a caring and just society.

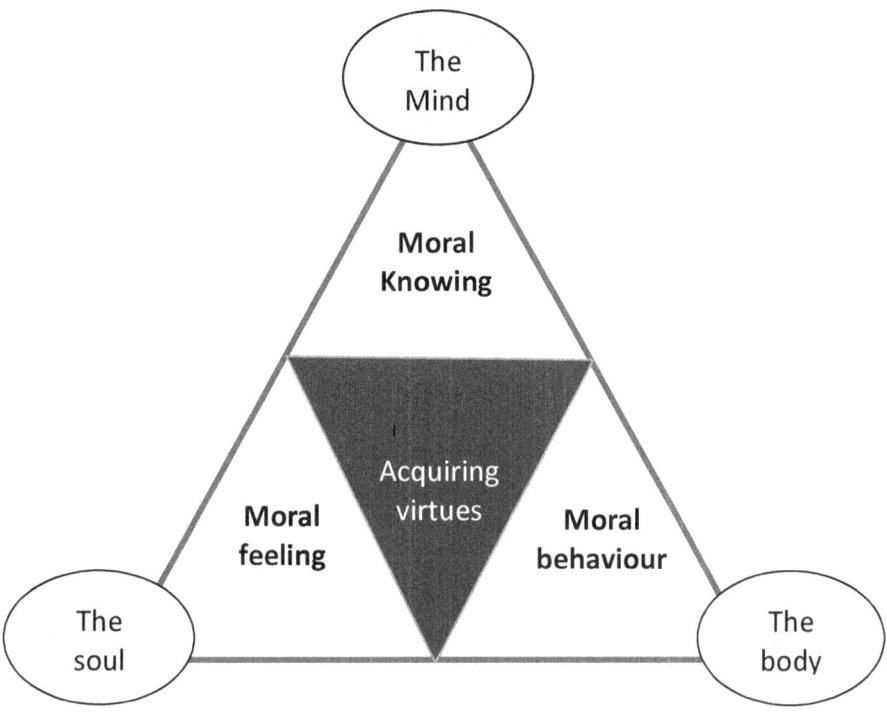

Figure 12.1 – The process of acquiring virtues

12.7 Activities

12.7.1 Double choice questions

Indicate whether each of the following statements is false or true.

		False	True
a)	Our first cell formed at the time of conception contains our complete spiritual characteristics.	☐	☐
b)	The human physical capacities exceed what an average person can achieve.	☐	☐
c)	Our intellectual capacities are only the potentials inherent in our brain.	☐	☐
d)	Our inner capacities should be developed and cultivated.	☐	☐
e)	Our inner capacities unfold as we grow older.	☐	☐
f)	Virtues are part of the mind's inner capacities.	☐	☐
g)	We can live happily without acquiring virtues.	☐	☐
h)	Virtues can significantly affect the quality and happiness of our lives.	☐	☐
i)	All that is needed to acquire a virtue is to develop a passion for it.	☐	☐
j)	What is needed to acquire a virtue is to learn about it, develop a passion for it, and then practice it.	☐	☐
k)	Our physical capacities unfold as we mature.	☐	☐
l)	Moral knowledge is increased by learning about a virtue.	☐	☐
m)	Moral feeling develops when we learn about a virtue.	☐	☐
n)	Moral behaviour automatically increases	☐	☐

as we grow up.
o) Virtues are about manifesting the gifts ☐ ☐
　　within us through our attitudes, words
　　and deeds.

12.7.2 Short answer questions

1. Consider the following quotation:

   "Regard man as a mine rich in gems of inestimable value ..."[1]

   a) Give three examples of *"gems of inestimable value"*.

   _____
   _____
   _____
   _____

   b) How easily can gems be extracted from mines?

   _____
   _____
   _____

   c) What are the gems within us?

   _____
   _____
   _____

   d) What is your overall understanding of the above quotation?

   _____
   _____
   _____
   _____

---

[1] Bahá'u'lláh, *Gleanings from the Writings of Bahá'u'lláh*, p. 260.

2. What is your understanding of physical capacities?

_____
_____
_____
_____

3. What is your understanding of intellectual capacities?

_____
_____
_____
_____

4. What is your understanding of spiritual capacities?

_____
_____
_____
_____

5. In the following table, the three realities of man are shown on the left and the three stages of acquiring virtues are given on the right. Draw connecting lines from the circle of each reality to the circle of the stage of acquiring virtues that is associated with it.

Physical reality ○	○	Moral Knowledge
Intellectual reality ○	○	Moral feeling
Spiritual reality ○	○	Moral behaviour

6. Consider the following story and answer the questions asked.

Aaliya started high school just a month ago. She is a relatively small girl with reddish hair. On the first day of school, while walking in the playground, an older boy approached her and started to tease her about her height and hair. She asked the boy to leave her alone. However, the boy continued to verbally abuse her to the extent that she started to cry. She was deeply disturbed by this experience.

During dinner, Aaliya's father noticed that she was not her usual happy self. He asked her what the matter was. Aaliya told him of her experience at school. Her Dad told her that she was the victim of bullying.

After dinner, Aaliya accessed the Internet to learn more about "bullying". She realized that one will only bully others or hurt them if one has no consideration or respect for their feelings. She strongly felt that she should never bully others. This experience helped Aaliya to develop a passion for the virtues of consideration and respect. From that day, Aaliya was more conscious of her relationships and interactions with others, and she did her best to treat them with respect and consideration.

a)   What part of the story refers to moral knowledge?

_____
_____
_____
_____

b)   What part of the story refers to moral feeling?

_____
_____
_____
_____

c)   What part of the story refers to moral behaviour?

_____
_____
_____
_____

7. Identify the best ways of developing moral knowledge about a virtue.

_____
_____

8. Identify the best ways of developing moral feeling for a virtue.

9. Identify the best ways of developing moral behaviour for a virtue.

12.7.3 Projects

1. Virtues shield: Make a virtues shield poster, similar to the one shown in Figure 12.2. On the poster write two of your strong virtues (core virtues), one weak virtue (challenge virtue), and what makes you joyful. In the centre of the shield, include a symbol or a logo that represents you.
2. Describe a personal experience in which you have used moral knowledge, feeling and behaviour to acquire a virtue.

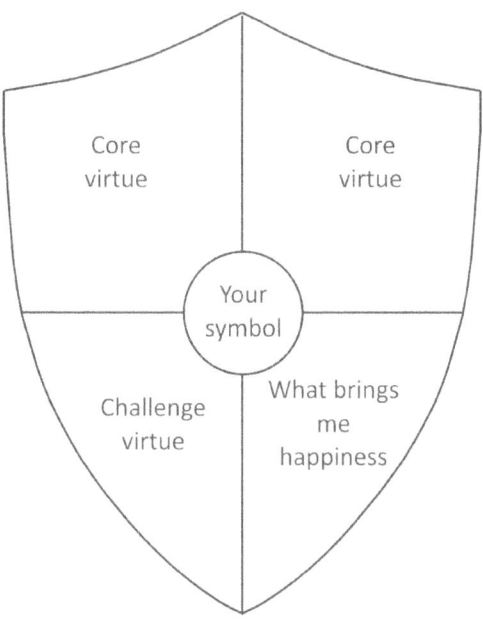

Figure 12.2 – Virtues shield

13 Free Will and Moral Choices

13.1 Introduction

Man is endowed with the gift to understand and perceive intellectual realities through the power of reasoning, and to make decisions through the mind in a process which involves the mental powers of the soul, the human spirit and the brain. Thus we, humans, are empowered to exercise our free will to make choices and, most importantly, to make moral choices. Every choice we make has direct or indirect consequences that affect us and the people around us. We are responsible for these choices and we should accept their consequences. In this chapter the concept of human free will be explored and its application in making moral choices will be explored. The role of our acquired virtues in making moral choices will be highlighted.

In this chapter, you need to reflect on and understand the following key points:

a) The animal is a captive of nature and only acts according to the requirements of its physical reality.
b) Man, through his understanding of the laws of the nature, has the ability to harness the forces of nature and to exceed the limitations dictated by it. However, man has no free will in some matters to do with his own physical nature.
c) The crucial aspect of human free will is in making choices between good or evil.
d) The process of making a decision to do good or evil is called making a moral choice.

e) It is possible to identify three categories of motivating forces driving a moral choice: avoiding punishment and receiving a reward, obeying the law and respecting human values, and the application of virtues.

13.2 Human free will

An animal is a captive of nature and acts only according to the requirements of its physical reality, whereas man can deviate from the natural laws and make choices. This is a major difference between man and the animal.

Since it lacks intellectual and spiritual realities, an animal blindly follows its instincts and desires. According to 'Abdu'l-Bahá, an animal *"... possesses no power of ideation or conscious intelligence; it is a captive of the senses and deprived of that which lies beyond them. It is subject to what the eye sees, the ear hears, the nostrils sense, the taste detects and touch reveals. These sensations are acceptable and sufficient for the animal."*[1] Consequently, an animal is ignorant of what is beyond its senses.

Obedience to the laws of nature is not just one of the characteristics of the animal but of the entire physical world, from large galaxies to infinitesimal particles such as electrons and protons in an atom. Only man, through his understanding of the laws of nature, has the ability to harness the forces of nature and surmount the limitations dictated by it. Scientific discoveries and inventions are exploited by man to develop methods and instruments, such as telecommunications systems, air transport and digital technology, to rule over nature.

The ability of man to reach a conclusion by applying reason to his mental powers is the primary tool in achieving his dominance over nature. Through this ability, man is also able to make choices when a moral issue is encountered. This is known as human free will and is recognized as another major difference between man and the animal.

13.3 Making moral choices

'Abdu'l-Bahá explains:

"Some things are subject to the free will of man, such as justice, equity, tyranny and injustice, in other words, good

---

[1] 'Abdu'l-Bahá, *Bahá'í World Faith*, p. 235.

and evil actions; it is evident and clear that these actions are, for the most part, left to the will of man. But there are certain things to which man is forced and compelled, such as sleep, death, sickness, decline of power, injuries and misfortunes; these are not subject to the will of man, and he is not responsible for them, for he is compelled to endure them. But in the choice of good and bad actions he is free, and he commits them according to his own will."[1]

For example, we can use our free will to make the following choices:

- Be compassionate towards our friends or to treat them with callousness.
- Be honest and trustworthy, or crafty and untrustworthy.
- Be loyal to our friends, or unfaithful and traitorous.
- Treat everyone with equity and justice irrespective of their appearance, colour, language or religion; or be unfair and unjust.

The process of making a decision to do good or evil is called making a moral choice. Every choice we make has direct or indirect consequences on the people around us. We are responsible for these choices and we should accept their consequences.

13.4 Moral motivations

Reflex reactions to intense sensory stimuli—for example removing our fingers from a very hot surface—are instantaneous and not driven by rational motivations. However, there are some decisions and judgments based on our sensory perceptions that are rational, for example putting on a warm jumper when we are feeling cold. In a more complex example, if we recognise from our symptoms that we have an infection, we may decide to take antibiotics as we know this will cure our illness. Our choice is based on a rational decision.

In contrast to purely rational choices, moral judgements are driven by emotional desires and moral motivations. It is possible to identify three categories of motivating forces driving moral choices. The first category of moral motivations is a fear of the social consequences of our choices and actions. For example, we do not cheat in an examination because we know that we might be caught, given a fail

---

[1] 'Abdu'l-Bahá, *Some Answered Questions*, p. 248.

mark for the subject and even expelled from school. We do not tease and abuse our classmates in the classroom because we know the teacher is very sensitive about this issue and it can get us into trouble. However, we may cheat if we are sure that we will not be caught. We may also tease our classmate if we find him/her alone outside the classroom.

Alternatively, we might base our moral choices on a need to satisfy our desire to receive approval of people that we respect or look up to.

At a more developed level, our choices are made on the basis of a belief in abstract, universal principles of right and wrong, or values. This represents the second category of moral motivation. For example, when we believe that cheating is unfair and unjust, we do not cheat in an examination under any circumstances. We also do not abuse or bully anyone since we genuinely respect other human beings and respect the basic rights of every individual. We are disturbed when they are distressed or in pain,

Thirdly, moral choices might be driven by virtues that are embedded in our character; and are automatically and genuinely manifested in our attitudes, words and deeds towards the people around us. For example, when we acquire the virtue of kindness, it becomes as second nature for us to show love and compassion towards other people in all our words and actions regardless of the circumstances, and we would not dream of ever displaying malice, hatred or aggression.

13.5 Moral development

The three categories of moral motivations described in section 13.4 represents different stages of moral development in an individual; and the roles that the physical, intellectual and spiritual selves play in making the choices.

In the first category, an individual makes a moral choice and takes an action mainly in obedience either to receive a reward or avoid punishment. In this situation, a moral choice is usually made when it satisfies the desires and needs of the individual. In this process, the physical self, and its instinctive behaviour to protect the self, play a significant role. This represents the first stage of moral development.

In this first stage, the ego, representing our animal side, strongly dominates our moral decision making. Our egocentric tendency protects self-interest in every decision made. Hence, if we think we are at risk of punishment, which we consider as harmful to the self, we will obey the rules; otherwise, we will ignore them. Our obedience may also stem from a hope of reward.

In the second stage, the individual may also have a concern for what people think of him when an action is taken, and there is the desire to receive group approval of the action. The correct moral choice is the one that pleases and impresses others. This can be further developed into a broader concern about society as a whole. Moral choices are made in order to obey laws, to respect authority, and to perform one's duties to society so that the social order is maintained. In this process, moral decisions are the result of thought processes where the intellectual self plays a major role. This can be considered as the second stage of moral development.

In the third category, an action is right when it is compatible with the virtues and spiritual principles embedded in the individual. The moral choices are made automatically in response to the experience of the individual without the need for much thought and rational reasoning. In this process the spiritual self plays the major role. This is the ultimate and ideal stage of moral development. Different stages of moral development are illustrated in Figure 13.1.

Acquisition of virtues is the unfolding of the powers potentially inherent in our spiritual reality. This is known as spiritual growth. As we embed more virtues in our habits, thoughts and attitudes; our spiritual reality plays a more dominant role in our moral decision making and, as a result, we operate more at the stage 3 level.

It is possible to assign specific age groupings to each stage of moral development based on the typical responses elicited by a moral dilemma. For example, stage 1 of moral development is considered by many scientists as the typical moral status of children around 7–10 years old. However, one cannot really generalize as there are also many older people who respond to a moral dilemma at a stage 1 level.

13.6 Heinz Dilemma

In order to illustrate the three stages of moral development, one of the scenarios used by Lawrence Kohlberg (1927–1987), known as the

Heinz Dilemma[1] will be described in this section with possible responses adapted to correspond to each aforementioned stage.

> "A woman was near death from a special kind of cancer. There was one drug that the doctors thought might save her. It was a form of radium that a druggist in the same town had recently discovered. The drug was expensive to make, but the druggist was charging ten times what the drug cost him to produce. He paid $200 for the radium and charged $2,000 for a small dose of the drug. The sick woman's husband, Heinz, went to everyone he knew to borrow the money, but he could only get together about $1,000 which is half of what it cost. He told the druggist that his wife was dying and asked him to sell it cheaper or let him pay later. But the druggist said: 'No, I discovered the drug and I'm going to make money from it.' So Heinz got desperate and broke into the man's store to steal the drug for his wife. Should Heinz have broken into the laboratory to steal the drug for his wife? Why or why not?"

- Stage 1 response:

  Heinz may be tempted to steal the drug, because he does not want to be left as a lonely widower when his wife dies. However he will probably decide not to risk being caught and sent to jail. He would find the punishment and the stigma of a criminal record unbearable. In both cases Heinz is being motivated by self-interest.

- Stage 2 response:

  Heinz is tempted to steal the drug because he loves his wife and does not want to her to suffer. He also thinks that he would win the approval of his in-laws who do not want to lose a beloved daughter. However, Heinz realises that, if caught, the enforcers of the law will not consider his wife's need as mitigation for the crime against the drug developer who spent many years of his life in creating the cure. Though some people may be sympathetic to him, Heinz knows that to steal is immoral and that those in authority will still view his action as criminal. At stage 2 level of

---

[1] Carol Gibb Harding (editor), *Moral Dilemmas and Ethical Reasoning*, Precedent Publishing, Inc., 1985.

his spiritual development, Heinz considers the moral dilemma mainly from an intellectual perspective.

- Stage 3 response

Although Heinz feels frustrated and sorrowful that he cannot buy the drug that would cure his beloved wife, the idea of stealing it does not even enter his mind. He has been finding spiritual solace in prayer throughout his wife's illness. Now, he and his wife pray together, imploring God to give them both, and all their family and friends, the strength to accept His will with grace. Heinz is exemplifying to what degree the virtues of honesty, detachment and trust in God's mercy have been embedded in his soul over the years.

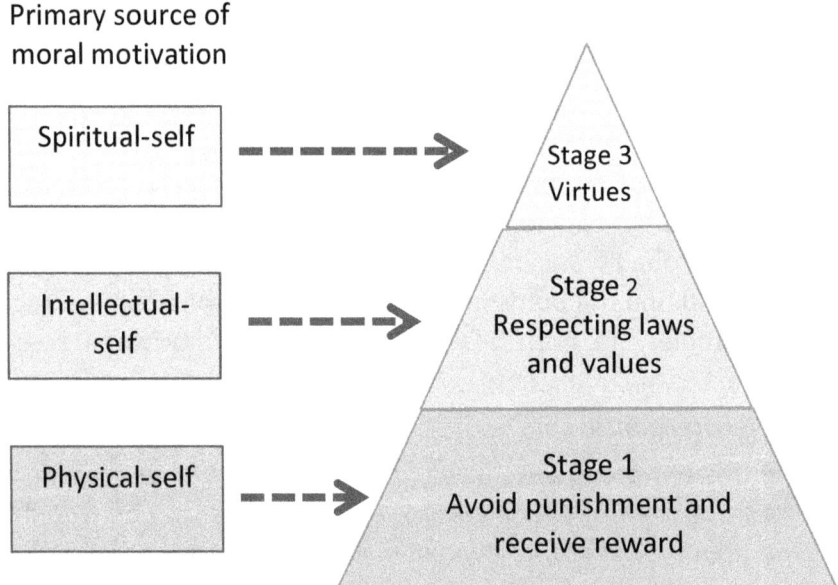

Figure 13.1 – Stages of moral development

13.7 Activities

13.7.1 Double choice questions

Indicate whether each of the following statements is false or true.

		False	True
a)	We have the ability to make moral choices.	☐	☐
b)	We always make our moral decisions because of our fear of the consequences.	☐	☐
c)	Our acquired virtues can affect our moral choices.	☐	☐
d)	Because I am kind, I am not inclined to tease or bully my classmates.	☐	☐
e)	In stage 1 of moral development, moral choices are made because of a belief in certain spiritual principles.	☐	☐
f)	In stage 2 of moral development, the correct moral choice is the one that pleases and impresses others.	☐	☐
g)	In stage 2 of moral development, the individual has a concern about what people think of him when an action is taken.	☐	☐
h)	In stage 3 of moral development, the right action is the one that respects and protects the rights of the individual according to the laws approved by society.	☐	☐
i)	Our physical-self has a strong influence on our moral choices in stage 1 of moral development.	☐	☐
j)	Our intellectual-self has a strong influence on our moral choices at stage 2 of moral development	☐	☐

k) Our spiritual-self has a strong influence on our moral choices in stage 3 of moral development. ☐ ☐

l) Our intellectual-self has a weak influence on our moral choices at stage 2 of moral development. ☐ ☐

m) Our physical-self has a weak influence on our moral choices at stage 3 of moral development. ☐ ☐

13.7.2 Short answer questions

1. What is meant by making moral choices?

2. What is the meaning of "human free will"?

3. Does man have free will for every choice?

4. What are moral motivations?

5. Describe the three categories of moral motivations.

6. What are the three stages of moral development?

7. How are the three stages of moral development associated with the physical-self, the intellectual-self and the spiritual-self?

8. Alice lives in a neighbourhood where there is a closely bonded group of teenagers. A new girl from overseas called Maryam has recently moved into the neighbourhood with her family. Maryam is quite shy and speaks broken English with a strange accent. She always wears a scarf with a long dress over a wide pair of pants. One day, when a close group of teenagers are hanging out, one of them, by the name of Tom, starts to criticize Maryam behind her back, making comments about how strange and different she is. He tells the others to stay away from Maryam as she is "very weird". Alice is not sure how to respond. She does not want to go against the wishes of Tom and the others. However, Alice thinks Tom is judging Maryam only by her appearance as he does not know Maryam well. Hence, his comments are not just and fair.

a) In your view, how should Alice react to Tom? Why?

___

b) What would be Maryam's response if she acts according to stage 1 of moral development?

___

c) What should be Maryam's response if she acts according to stage 2 of moral development?

___

d) What should be Maryam's response if she acts according to stage 3 of moral development?

___

e) What virtues help Maryam to give an effective response in stage 3 of moral development? A list of virtues are provided in Appendix A of this chapter.

___

13.7.3 Project

Reflect on the state of your moral development and describe it in about 200 words. You should consider the following points:

a) According to what stage of moral development do you usually make your moral choices?
b) Mention some examples of your past choices that support the judgement you have made about yourself in (a).
c) What is your ideal stage of moral development?
d) How are you going to reach this stage?

13.8 Appendix A - Selected list of virtues

Assertiveness	To be positive and confident
Caring	Showing love and attention to people and things that matter to you
Cleanliness	To wash often, keeping your body clean and wearing clean clothes (purity)
Compassion	Understanding and caring about someone who is in trouble or has made a mistake
Confidence	Self-assurance; an honest and realistic appreciation of ones abilities; (especially when supported by prayerfulness and trust in God).
Consideration	To have regard for other people and their feelings (kindness, thoughtfulness)
Courage	Personal bravery in the face of fear (boldness, heroism)
Courtesy	To be polite and to have good manners (chivalry, civility, politeness)
Creativity	The way you use your special combination of gifts and talents (inventiveness, resourcefulness, wit)
Detachment	To experience your feelings without allowing them to control you
Determination	Firmness of purpose; e.g. focusing your energy and efforts on a particular task, and sticking to it until it is done (resoluteness)
Enthusiasm	Doing something whole-heartedly (eagerness, fervour, zeal)
Excellence	Doing your best (merit)
Faithfulness	Being true to someone or something (trustworthiness, loyalty, truthfulness)
Flexibility	Being open to the need for change (adaptability)

Forgiveness	Overlooking the mistakes others make and loving them just as much as before (benignity)
Friendliness	Taking an interest in other people, making them feel welcome, and being willing to share with them (affection, amicability, cordiality, pleasantness, devotion, love)
Generosity	Sharing (liberality, munificence)
Gentleness	Acting and speaking in a way that is considerate and kind to others
Helpfulness	Being of service to someone (giving assistance, making oneself useful)
Honesty	Being sincere, open, trustworthy and truthful (integrity, purity, veracity)
Honour	To live with a sense of respect for what you believe to be right (esteem, loyalty, respect)
Humility	To be humble (self-effacement, meekness, modesty, submission)
Idealism	To care about what is right and meaningful in life (perfection)
Joyfulness	To be filled with happiness, peace, love, and a sense of well-being (gladness)
Justice	To be fair in everything you do (equity, fairness, righteousness)
Kindness	Being concerned about the welfare of others (benevolence, charity, love, thoughtfulness, warmth)
Love	Caring for someone, wanting to be near them, and wanting to share with them (admiration, affection, warmth)
Loyalty	Standing up for something you believe in, and having unwavering faith (allegiance, devotion, constancy, fidelity, truthfulness)
Mercy	Giving people more than they deserve, whereas justice is giving them what they deserve (clemency, compassion, grace,

	leniency)
Moderation	Not going to extremes; not taking more than you need, or more than is good for you; using neither too much nor too little; (frugality, temperance)
Modesty	Not overestimating ones abilities or achievements; having a sense of self-respect; avoiding indecency or impropriety in ones behaviour or dress; (humility, simplicity)
Obedience	To follow what is right, listening to what your parents and others in authority have to say and doing it as faithfully as you can (compliance, respect)
Orderliness	Being neat, and living with a sense of harmony; being methodical; (neatness, thoroughness, regularity)
Patience	Having quiet hope and expectation based on trust that, in the end, everything will be all right (forbearance, perseverance, composure, resignation)
Peacefulness	Having a sense of inner calm that can come in moments of silent gratitude or prayer (calmness, harmony, placidity, quietude, serenity)
Prayerfulness	Living always with the awareness that you are in the presence of your Creator
Purposefulness	Having a good reason for doing something and sticking to it despite distractions
Reliability	Doing something that you have agreed to do in a predictable way (dependability, trustworthiness)

14 Self-respect

14.1 Introduction

The focus of this chapter is on self-respect and self-worth. In the previous chapter, we learned that we have the ability to make choices when faced with a moral situation or dilemma. Many moral decisions relate directly or indirectly to our "self"; either the physical-self, the intellectual-self or the spiritual-self. In this chapter the nature and characteristics of the moral choices that reflect our respect for the three aspects of our "self" will be explored.

In this chapter you need to reflect on and understand the following key points:

a) Self-respect is the care and attention we give to our own self.
b) Self-respect means we have a positive attitude towards ourselves because of who we are and the capacities we have.
c) Self-respect requires an equal and balanced attention to all our three realities—the physical-self, the intellectual-self and the spiritual-self.
d) The best sign of respect for our physical-self is to minimize harm to our body and to keep it healthy.
e) Respect for our intellectual-self means taking care of our mind so that it can work efficiently and effectively.
f) Respecting the spiritual-self requires the strengthening of our perfections, the qualities hidden in our spiritual-self, to the extent that they overcome the temptations and dominance of our imperfections or of our physical self.

14.2 Self-respect

Respect is a crucial virtue that is reflected in our attitudes to ourselves and others. We respect people when we care about them and treat them with honour. Respect leads to more dignified relationships with others. It also helps us to treat our home, school and environment with reverence.

Self-respect is the care and attention we give to our own self. As human beings, we are born noble with many inner capacities and gifts. All our three realities (physical, intellectual and spiritual) have enormous powers and potentialities. Appreciating these powers, striving to cultivate and develop them, and caring for them, are all intrinsic parts of self-respect. Overall, respect is the ability to see and celebrate the values in ourselves and others. 'Abdu'l-Bahá states that self-respect is the foundation of *"man's supreme honour and real happiness"*.[1]

Self-respect for ourselves means that we value ourselves regardless of our successes or failures, or our perceived inferiority or superiority with respect to others. We simply appreciate ourselves because of who we are and the capacities we have.

Self-respect requires an equal and balanced attention to our "self" including the physical-self, the intellectual-self and the spiritual-self. Here are some examples:

- Respecting the physical-self:
    - I eat well by avoiding junk food.
    - I exercise regularly.
    - I get sufficient sleep.
    - I look after my health.
    - I do not harm my body by using alcohol, drugs and other harmful substances.
    - I keep myself and my environment clean.
- Respecting the intellectual-self:
    - I make use of every opportunity to learn.
    - I treat my school work seriously.
    - I am diligent in doing my school homework.
    - I strive to improve my analytical skills.

---

[1] 'Abdu'l-Bahá, *The Secret of Divine Civilization*, p. 19.

- ➢ I do not take harmful substances that may damage my brain.
- Respecting the spiritual-self:
  - ➢ I try to avoid anxiety and stress.
  - ➢ I am conscious of my virtues.
  - ➢ I try to maintain good relationships with the people around me.
  - ➢ I work on improving my challenge virtues.
  - ➢ I avoid backbiting and gossip.
  - ➢ I am kind, truthful, trustworthy and honest.

14.3 Respecting the physical-self

Our physical self is a very complex system. The physical body is the component of the physical-self that supports the intellectual and spiritual selves. In the same way as any complex machine, our physical body needs to be well looked after and treated with the utmost care. The best sign of respect for our physical-self is to minimize harm to our body and to keep it healthy.

Care and respect for our body can in some ways be compared to the care we give to our car. We know that our car will only run efficiently if we supply it with the correct fuel. It also needs to be regularly serviced. If the engine lubricants are of the wrong type, too little or too dirty; or the filters are not clean; then the engine will not run efficiently. This will lead to increased wear of some parts of the engine and eventually it will stop. We should also clean, polish and protect the body and interior of the car in an effort to keep it in good condition for as long as possible.

When it comes to our physical self, our health depends on what we consume and how we look after our body. Our vital organs—our brain, lungs and liver—play a major role in our survival. They are quite sensitive to harmful substances and are damaged by smoking, alcohol and harmful drugs. Hence, our decisions on what we eat or drink can significantly affect the health of our physical-self—it is also an indication of our respect for ourselves.

Unfortunately, many negative forces in our society such as media pressure, misleading advertising, and coercion from peers encourage us to abandon our self-respect and to engage in bad habits such as smoking, drinking and substance abuse, which have a directly adverse effect on our well-being and health.

14.4 Respecting the intellectual-self

Our intellectual-self is an important element of being human. As mentioned in the previous chapters, it primarily differentiates us from the animal by giving us the power of abstract thought, reasoning and decision making.

The power of our intellectual-self is manifested through the mind. Although scientists have not understood how the mind works, they believe the brain plays a major role in the operation of the mind. Our five external senses—sight, hearing, touch, taste and smell—provide sensory information to the brain. The brain processes this information and passes its perceptions to the mind . We refer to this it as sensory perception. With the help of the powers of our spiritual-self such as thought, understanding and memory, the mind interprets and extrapolates these stimuli. In our mind we make decisions, develop abstract thoughts and learn. This learning appears as a new understanding for future decision making.

Our choices and their consequences significantly affect the quality of our life and our happiness. Hence, it is critical that we ensure our mind is sound, can make good judgements and reach decisions that are conducive to our well-being.

Respecting our intellectual-self means taking care of our mind so that it can work efficiently and effectively. It also requires challenging our mind and brain to cultivate, develop and manifest the capacities inherent in them. This can be achieved by:

- Abstaining from substances that can harm our brain
- Taking an interest in discoveries and inventions.
- Exploring new learning opportunities.
- Reading a wide range of publications.
- Joining organizations that we have an interest in, such as an art or music society; or some other inspirational youth or school club.
- Having intellectual conversations or debates with our friends and classmates
- Learning a new language.
- Making friends with people from completely different backgrounds and learning about their lives and culture.
- Traveling in a foreign country.

14.5 Respecting the spiritual-self

An important initial step in respecting our spiritual-self is to recognize our station as a human being and identify the distinctive differences between us and other creatures.

Bahá'u'lláh states that we have been created noble and we must cultivate our inner capacities and gifts to achieve the potential we were created for.[1] According to 'Abdu'l-Bahá: *"Man is in the highest degree of materiality, and at the beginning of spirituality; that is to say, he is the end of imperfection and the beginning of perfection. ... meaning that he is the sum of all the degrees of imperfection, and that he possesses the degrees of perfection. He has the animal side as well as the angelic side; and the aim of an educator is to so train human souls, that their angelic aspect may overcome their animal side. Then, if the divine power in man which is his essential perfection, overcomes the satanic power, which is absolute imperfection, he becomes the most excellent among the creatures; but if the satanic power overcomes the divine power, he becomes the lowest of the creatures."*[2]

Respecting the spiritual-self requires the strengthening of our perfections—those qualities hidden in our spiritual-self—to the extent that they overcome the temptations and dominance of the imperfections of our physical self. In the next section, we will explore practical ways to achieve the nobility inherent within us.

The quality of the choices we make reflects the quality of our spiritual-self. Our inner capacities and virtues, when developed and cultivated, affect our thoughts and understanding. They influence our mind and its activities in a positive way. In addition, virtues help us to develop better relationships with the people around us. Good relationships, in turn, further enhance our thoughts and understanding.

Understanding the purpose of our life is another vital aspect of respecting our spiritual-self. We need to know how and why our life is important, and what are the things that matter the most. In addition, we need to pay attention to the fundamental questions that permeate our lives. We have an urge to know the meaning of our life, our

---

[1] Bahá'u'lláh, *The Hidden Words*, Arabic No. 22.
[2] 'Abdu'l-Bahá, *Bahá'í World Faith*, pp. 331–332.

origin, our destination, the meaning of death and the many other similar questions, which we should not ignore.

Our vision of the future and our hope to reach that vision can be a strong driving force in our lives. It gives us a reason to act and to cultivate our capacities to achieve the vision. It can also re-energise us when we are ready to give up.

Hence, we respect our spiritual-self when we cultivate our inner capacities towards achieving our goals and visions. This can be achieved by:

- Developing a high vision and goals for our life.
- Identifying our weak virtues and striving to improve them.
- Volunteering to work for a community project. Service to others helps us to develop perfections.
- Reading inspiring books about those who overcame their challenges.
- Listening to a friend in need of help.
- Doing something selfless and considerate each day.
- Reflecting on our convictions, and meditating on our "self", and what we feel life is about.

14.6 Activities

14.6.1 Double choice questions

Indicate whether each of the following statements is false or true.

		False	True
a)	The mind is dependent on the brain to operate.	☐	☐
b)	We fully understand the nature of the mind.	☐	☐
c)	Our thoughts have no effect on our mind.	☐	☐
d)	Our virtues help us to develop positive thoughts.	☐	☐
e)	Our understanding improves as we learn more.	☐	☐
f)	Our virtues determine the quality of our spiritual-self.	☐	☐
g)	Our spiritual-self can develop by doing advanced mathematics.	☐	☐
h)	Service and voluntary work can enhance our spiritual-self.	☐	☐
i)	The quality of our relationships with others has no impact on our self.	☐	☐
j)	Meditation and reflection can improve our physical-self.	☐	☐
k)	Man is created noble.	☐	☐
l)	It is guaranteed that every human being will become noble.	☐	☐
m)	Nobility is a potential within us and should be cultivated.	☐	☐

14.6.2 Reflecting on the "self"

Complete the following statements.

1. My favourite pass-time is _____.
2. I am generally _____ to my parents.

3. I am generally _____ to my friends.
4. I am generally _____ to my teachers.
5. I am generally _____ to strangers.
6. My health is _____ for me.
7. The things I like the best about my physical-self are:
   _____
8. The things I like the best about my intellectual-self are:
   _____
9. The things I like the best about my spiritual-self are:
   _____
10. The most important things in my life are _____
    _____.
11. I like to _____ as my hobby.
12. My favourite book _____.
13. I would like to do a course on _____
    _____ if I get the opportunity.
14. I like to _____ club in the school.
15. I _____ make new friends.
16. I am passionate about _____.
17. Learning a new language _____.
18. I am usually _____ to improve my mind.
19. My thoughts are mostly _____.
20. My understanding _____ over the last two years.
21. I _____ aware of my challenge virtues.
22. I _____ work as a service volunteer.
23. Meditation and reflection can _____
    _____.
24. My friends _____ to me about their problems.

25. Helping a friend with his homework _____ a selfless act.
26. Cleaning the house to help mum _____ a selfless act.
27. I think the purpose of this life is _____.
_____.
28. My main purpose in life is _____.
_____.
29. My heart is filled up with joy when I think about _____
_____.

14.6.3 Short answer questions

1. What is the meaning of self-respect?

2. What are the main characteristics of respecting the physical-self?

3. What are the main characteristics of respecting the intellectual-self?

4. What are the main characteristics of respecting the spiritual-self?

5. How can we achieve respect for our physical-self?
_____
_____
_____

6. How can we achieve respect for our intellectual-self?
_____
_____
_____

7. How can we achieve respect for our spiritual-self?
_____
_____
_____
_____

14.6.4 Assessing your "self"

Choose the most appropriate response to each statement.

1. Lack of self-confidence leads us to _____.
    a) feel timid in new situations.
    b) fear having new friends
    c) boast
    d) bully others
    e) all of the above
2. Virtues help us to _____.
    a) make better choices
    b) have better relationships with others
    c) feel happier
    d) all of the above
3. I respect my intellectual-self when I _____.
    a) eat healthy food
    b) abstain from substances harmful to my brain
    c) regularly exercise
    d) have good relationships with my friends

e) all of the above
4. I should respect myself because I _____.
   a) have great potentials
   b) am created noble
   c) can develop capabilities to serve others
   d) all of the above
5. Low self-esteem is a hindrance since it _____.
   a) makes us shy
   b) prevents us to achieve our full potential
   c) keep us from making friends
6. High self-esteem _____.
   a) affects how we live and how we relate to others
   b) is only appropriate for famous actors, athletes and politicians
   c) makes a person self-centred
7. If we do not have a capability in a given area, we could _____.
   a) be wasting time by working hard to develop a capability in that area
   b) improve our capabilities in that area through effort and practice
   c) forget about trying to build capability because we will never excel in that area
8. In order to develop a capability, we must _____.
   a) recognize our talents and spend time improving them
   b) be encouraged by parents, friends and teachers
   c) take private lessons
9. Long term goals _____.
   a) help us work toward achieving what we want out of life
   b) are not useful because they are too far in the future
   c) should not be planned because they are not specific enough
10. Short term goals _____.
    a) are not important enough to plan
    b) can be used to reach long-term goals
    c) are more important than long term goals.

14.6.5 Project

In this project you will be setting long term goals for your physical-self, intellectual-self and spiritual-self. For every long term goal, set one short term goal (milestone) towards achieving the long term goal. For the "method" describe how you are going to achieve your milestone. For "when", state specific time(s) that you are going to apply the method.

Here is an example:

- Long term goal for intellectual-self:

    Achieve a "B" grade in mathematics this term
- Milestone:

    Achieve at least a "B" grade in every weekly test
- Method:

    Study mathematics for 45 minutes a day, four days a week.
- When:

    Monday through Thursday evenings from 7:00 to 7:45 pm

Section III – Cultivating inner capacities

15 PURPOSE OF HUMAN LIFE

15.1 Introduction

Everything in the world of existence, whether man-made or natural, has a purpose. The meaning and purpose of human life have been the topic of many deep philosophical, scientific, and religious studies and discussions throughout human history. The responses to these questions, though many, can be categorised into two main groups: the materialistic and the spiritual perspectives. The materialistic response argues that human life has no high purpose; whereas in the spiritual perspective, the purpose of life is defined as an opportunity to develop the innate gifts and capacities. The focus of this chapter is to explore these perspectives.

In this chapter, you need to reflect on and understand the following key points:

a) The materialistic perspective suggests that human life has no high purpose.
b) The materialistic perspective denies the spiritual reality of man and the capacities associated with it.
c) The spiritual perspective suggests that the primary purpose of physical life is for individuals to develop their hidden gifts and capacities.
d) The capacities developed in the three realities of man should contribute towards the spiritual development of the individual and the progress of an ever-advancing human civilization.

15.2 Purposefulness of the universe

Everything in the world of existence, whether man-made or natural, has a purpose. For example, the primary purpose of a chair is to provide a support for someone to sit down on. If a chair does not serve its purpose, either because it is broken or uncomfortable, then it is discarded. A car is made to provide transportation. If a car is not functional, being either completely broken down or irreparably damaged, then it is scrapped.

In previous chapters, we stated that animals only have a physical reality. The capacities and functions of physical reality are sensory perception, growth and reproduction. The primary purpose of the life of an animal is to grow and reproduce to ensure the continuity of its species. The faculties possessed by an animal assist it in fulfilling this purpose. For example, sensory perception is used to gather food and to avoid danger. Hence, animals fulfil their purpose by utilising their capacities and powers.

Man, on the other hand, has a complex nature consisting of three realities: physical, intellectual and spiritual. These realities exist from the time of conception and are endowed with many hidden gifts and capacities. Since man's innate capacities and gifts are far superior to those of animals, it is logical to assume that man has a much greater responsibility, and should strive to fulfil a purpose that is well beyond the purpose of animals. It is natural to question why man has such a complex and unique nature. Is there a special purpose for the life of man? How should the innate gifts and capacities of man be used to achieve this purpose?

Questions regarding the meaning and purpose of human life have been the topic of many deep philosophical, scientific, and religious studies and discussions throughout human history. Although, there are many responses to these questions from various cultural, ideological and religious backgrounds, they can be categorised into two groups: materialistic and spiritual perspectives. We will look at these perspectives in the remainder of this chapter.

15.3 Materialistic perspective

The materialistic perspective only recognizes the physical reality of man and suggests that the intellectual and spiritual characteristics manifested by man are simply the products of his physical reality. In other words, the mind and the spiritual powers of the soul are considered as by-products of the brain. However, no logical explanation nor scientific proof is provided to substantiate such assumptions.

To a great extent such views undermine the spiritual reality of man and his capacities and powers. In societies dominated by the materialistic perspective, little effort is made either to develop the spiritual capacities of the citizens or to provide opportunities for the people to draw on their spiritual qualities to contribute to the development of the society. Self-centredness and self-love are the main characteristics of such societies and the people largely have very noisy egos.

In addition, the materialistic perspective implies that man is no more than a conscious animal driven by instinctive forces such as self-protection, self-survival and domination. There is no higher purpose to life. The primary objective of human life is to go through life with as much pleasure and as little suffering as possible. There is no potential nor need for self-development and spiritual transformation.

In an individual where the capacities of the three realities are equally developed, the mind to some extent regulates the more extreme instinctive behaviours of the physical reality using the power and influence of the spiritual reality. However, in an individual with a strong higher self, the power of the mind and intellect will be fully in charge of the instinctive behaviour of man's lower nature.

Wild animals such as lions are ferocious in their struggle to catch and kill their prey because of their carnivorous nature. However, the ferocity of man stems from selfishness, greed and oppression. That is why man can be much more dangerous than wild animals if he does not cultivate his spiritual capacities. In this regard, 'Abdu'l-Bahá states:

> *"If the animals are savage and ferocious, it is simply a means for their subsistence and preservation. They are deprived of that degree of intellect which can reason and discriminate between right and wrong, justice and injustice; they are justified in their actions and not responsible. When man is ferocious and cruel toward his fellowman, it is not for subsistence or safety. His motive is selfish advantage and wilful wrong. It is neither seemly nor befitting that such a*

noble creature, endowed with intellect and lofty thoughts, capable of wonderful achievements and discoveries in sciences and arts, with potential for ever higher perceptions and the accomplishment of divine purposes in life, should seek the blood of his fellowmen upon the field of battle."[1]

Past and current human history clearly shows that individuals who have been captives to their physical-self and the lower nature have perpetrated atrocities and cruelties that no animal would commit.

15.4 Spiritual perspective

The core of the spiritual perspective is that the purpose of life is defined as an opportunity for individuals to develop their innate gifts and capacities. As mentioned previously, our three realities (physical, intellectual and spiritual) have hidden gifts. The developed capacities should be deployed towards the advancement of two major processes: the spiritual development of the individual and the advancement of human material and spiritual civilization.

15.4.1 Contributing to spiritual development

The first process is the spiritual development of the individual. This occurs when the capacities of the spiritual reality are cultivated and developed within the human soul.

Since the soul and the qualities within it are non-tangible and beyond the influence of matter, they are not governed by physical laws. This means that the soul and its qualities survive the death of the physical body and continue to develop in the next world. The degree of the soul's progress after physical death is dependent on the extent to which the spiritual qualities are developed within the individual during his physical life.

Although spiritual progress occurs within the soul, the physical experiences gained by living in the material world and the interactions with other individuals play a major role in this process. The effectiveness of these experiences in advancing the process of spiritual growth depends on how successfully an individual has cultivated his capacities within the intellectual and physical realities.

Hence, contrary to the materialistic perspective, the spiritual perspective considers the development of the innate spiritual gifts

---

[1] 'Abdu'l-Bahá, *The Promulgation of Universal Peace*, p. 352.

and capacities as the primary purpose of physical life. This is achieved through the collective operation and interaction of the three realities of man.

15.4.2 Contributing to an ever-advancing civilization

The word civilization has its roots in the Latin adjective *civilis*, a reference to a citizen. Citizens in a society endeavour to work within political, social, economic and religious organizations as part of an integrated larger community. As a part of this process, a civilization facilitates the development of a particular shared way of thinking about the world that is reflected in the art, literature, drama and a host of other cultural activities of that civilization.

Over the last 6,000 years of recorded history, many civilizations have come into existence and later disappeared. Each has added to the collective human heritage by their advancements in science, technology, arts and literature. Such advancements are the result of the contributions of individuals living in those societies.

Bahá'u'lláh has stated that:

"All men have been created to carry forward an ever advancing civilization."[1]

Thus individuals in every society should cultivate and develop their inner capacities, and contribute their talents and skills towards advancing human civilization. This is a purpose for the physical life of an individual.

However, the higher purpose of life is to advance divine or spiritual civilization:

"Bahá'u'lláh teaches that material civilization is incomplete, insufficient and that divine civilization must be established. Material civilization concerns the world of matter or bodies, but divine civilization is the realm of ethics and moralities. Until the moral degree of the nations is advanced and human virtues attain a lofty level, happiness for mankind is impossible."[2]

---

[1] Bahá'u'lláh, *Gleanings from the Writings of Bahá'u'lláh*, p. 215.
[2] 'Abdu'l-Bahá, *The Promulgation of Universal Peace*, p. 375.

15.5 Activities

15.5.1 Double choice questions

For each statement given below, determine whether it has a materialistic perspective (MP) or a spiritual view (SP):

		MP	SP
a)	There is no higher purpose to life.	☐	☐
b)	The primary purpose of physical life is for the individuals to develop their innate gifts and capacities.	☐	☐
c)	Our innate capacities should be developed and cultivated during our physical life.	☐	☐
d)	Man has only one reality.	☐	☐
e)	The mind and the spiritual powers of the soul are considered to be by-products of the brain.	☐	☐
f)	The soul, and its qualities, survives the death of the physical body and continues its progress.	☐	☐
g)	The innate spiritual gifts and capacities are developed through the collective operation and interaction of the three realities of man.	☐	☐
h)	The degree of the progress made by the soul after physical death is dependent on the extent to which the spiritual qualities are developed within the individual during physical life.	☐	☐
i)	Man is no more than a conscious animal driven by instinctive forces such as self-protection, self-survival and domination.	☐	☐
j)	The primary objective of human life is to go through life with as much pleasure and as little suffering as possible.	☐	☐
k)	There is no potential for self-development and spiritual transformation in man.	☐	☐

l) The power of the mind and intellect of an individual with undeveloped spiritual capacities will be fully under the control of instinctive behaviour and the lower nature of man. ☐ ☐

15.5.2 Short answer questions

1. Does nature have a purpose? Explain.
   _____
   _____
   _____
   _____

2. What are the main points of the materialistic perspective on the purpose of life?
   _____
   _____
   _____
   _____

3. Under what condition(s) does man become more dangerous than an animal?
   _____
   _____
   _____
   _____

4. What is the purpose of life according to the spiritual perspective?
   _____
   _____
   _____
   _____

5. What is spiritual development?

6. Why is spiritual development important for every human being?

7. How can the three realities of man collectively assist in realizing the spiritual development of an individual?

8. What is your understanding of the term an "ever advancing civilization"?

9. How can an individual contribute towards an "ever advancing civilization"?

10. The following four hypothetical scenarios are designed to examine your understanding of the content of this chapter. Identify, and comment on, what each of the depicted teenagers understands to be the purpose of life.

   a) Annette's ambition in life is to be a nurse. She loves to help people. This will enable her to help those who really need help.

   _____
   _____
   _____
   _____

   b) John believes that life is about having a good time and enjoying the best of everything that life offers. He would work hard to earn sufficient money to afford such a life style.

   _____
   _____
   _____
   _____

   c) Adam's ambition in life is to be a teacher. He likes the job and also it provides him with the opportunity to educate the next generation. He believes this will be a great contribution to his society.

   _____
   _____
   _____
   _____

   d) Jasmine is determined to realize her full potential and to excel in everything. Her struggle is not a competition against others, but against her own self.

   _____
   _____

15.5.3 Project

In this project, you will be reflecting on the purpose of life. The following questions guide you in this process. Summarize your responses in a poster.

a) In your opinion, which perspective results in a better society: a spiritual or a materialistic one? Explain your reasons.
b) What is your ambition in life? Consider it in the context of the profession that you would love to be trained for and pursue. If you have not made up your mind yet, choose a profession to match your ambition.
c) Comment on this ambition in the context of a spiritual and a materialistic perspective on the purpose of life.

16 Knowledge, Volition, Action

16.1 Introduction

Unveiling inner capacities is dependent on both personal endeavour as well as assistance from others. The focus of this chapter is on a practical strategy that can assist us to realize our innate potentials. This strategy consists of the three major steps of knowledge, volition and action. We will explore how this approach can be applied in cultivating the capacities hidden within our physical, intellectual and spiritual realities.

In this chapter, you need to reflect on and understand the following key points:

a) Unveiling inner capacities is dependent on both personal endeavour and help from others.
b) The inner gifts can be developed through pursuing the three steps of knowledge, volition and action.
c) Knowledge is the acquiring of a better understanding of our physical, intellectual and spiritual selves, the capacities we are endowed with, and specific methods that can be applied to cultivate them.
d) Volition is the process of developing a desire and strong will to realize our capacities.
e) Action is the process of implementing the necessary steps in developing our capacities.

16.2 A strategy for personal effort

Our inner gifts and capacities cannot be realized unless they are cultivated and developed through our systematic efforts and a great deal of commitment. This is true even in the physical world. A priceless gem will not show its brilliance and value until it is polished through the tireless efforts of a craftsman. Otherwise, it will look like any other stone.

Unfoldment of the inner capacities is dependent on both personal endeavours and help from others. Our parents, teachers and friends play their roles in empowering us to reach our potentials. This development is more effective when it is supported by our systematic personal efforts.

'Abdu'l-Bahá describes an effective strategy for attaining a goal. He states:

"The attainment of any object is conditioned upon knowledge, volition and action. Unless these three conditions are forthcoming there is no execution or accomplishment. In the erection of a house it is first necessary to know the ground and design the house suitable for it; second, to obtain the means or funds necessary for the construction; third, to actually build it."[1]

Hence, in order to systematically set about realizing our inner gifts, we need to embark on the three steps of knowledge, volition and action.

To gain knowledge, we need to acquire a better understanding of our physical, intellectual and spiritual selves; the capacities that they are endowed with; and explore how we can cultivate these capacities.

Volition is the process of developing a desire and strong will for cultivating our capacities. Without a strong desire, we will not persevere when we are faced with challenges and difficulties, and consequently we will not succeed.

Action is the process of taking the practical steps necessary to unfold our capacities. In this stage we have to apply what we have learned in the first step.

In the following sections, we shall explore how the dynamics of knowledge, volition and action can be applied to realize our physical, intellectual and spiritual capacities. The discussion provides only one view on how knowledge, volition and action can be applied to develop

---

[1] 'Abdu'l-Bahá, *Foundations of World Unity*, p. 100.

our physical, intellectual and spiritual capacities. You can identify other perspectives through personal research and reflection.

16.3 Cultivating physical capacities

Cultivation of physical capacities is concerned with the development of the physical body and its potentialities. This can be achieved through the following steps:

- **Knowledge**: It is critical that we have a good understanding of our physical body. The knowledge gained about its functions and needs helps us to make better decisions about how to look after our body and develop it more effectively. We should also learn about what constitutes a good, nutritious diet as well as which foods we should avoid.
- **Volition**: We need to have a strong desire and will to develop our physical body. Without volition, we will not make a sustained effort towards achieving the goals we have set to cultivate our physical capacities.
- **Action**: At this stage, we actively pursue the task of developing our physical capacities and take the necessary actions to achieve it. It is possible to identify the following practical steps in the process of action:
    a) **Nourishment:** The cells in our body constantly require energy to do their tasks and also to replicate in order to repair and develop the tissues they constitute. Hence, we need to provide them with food and oxygen. Without proper nourishment the body cannot function and cells start to disintegrate and die.
    b) **Physical exercise**: As discussed in the previous chapters, the inner capacities of the physical body are unveiled through physical exercise. For example, through effective cardio training, we can improve our stamina and resilience. This enables us to work more effectively and efficiently, and to achieve more in our daily lives.
    c) **Application:** Having developed healthy habits of good nutrition and regular exercise to improve our strength and stamina, we should put our well-developed, fit and healthy bodies to work for our own benefit and the benefit of society; otherwise our efforts will have served little useful purpose—other than just looking and feeling good.

16.4 Cultivating intellectual capacities

Cultivation of intellectual capacities is concerned with the unveiling of the potentialities hidden in our intellectual reality and the mind. This is achieved through the following steps:

- **Knowledge**: We need to develop a good understanding of the nature of our mind, its inherent powers and how it functions. This will enable us to develop and enhance these powers more effectively and purposefully. We should identify which career or profession would suit our talents and aspirations while also fulfilling our love to serve humanity. We should use this knowledge to determine what studies and training we should undertake to achieve our goal.

- **Volition**: Pursuit of our intellectual and professional goals requires strong determination and resolve. This will occur when we have fully reflected on our goals and plans, and fully understood the role they play in fulfilling our aspirations and purpose in life. Learning about the lives of people who have contributed to society and served humanity through their intellectual endeavours can be a strong motivation for us.

- **Action**: Formal education currently provides the main source of nourishment and education of our intellectual reality. The primary focus of schools and universities is to develop the human intellectual capacities. Hence, during our formal education we should strive for excellence in our studies and do our best to produce the best outcome. Subjects such as mathematics, science and language are critical for the development of our mind and of enhancing our power of reasoning. Hence, we need to pay special attention to them.

16.5 Cultivating spiritual capacities

Cultivation of spiritual capacities is concerned with developing the potentialities hidden in our soul. This can be achieved through the following steps

- **Knowledge**: Though not a sufficient condition, increased knowledge is a necessary step towards attainment of spiritual development. It is important that we know what spiritual development is, why we should develop spiritually and how it can be achieved. We should also be aware of our spiritual status, and our spiritual strengths and shortcomings.

- **Volition**: An important step in the process of spiritual development is to acquire a thirst for spirituality. Volition is manifested through goal setting, perseverance, patience and resisting distractions. Acquiring knowledge of our true purpose in life will stimulate and encourage us to set spiritual goals for ourselves towards attaining that purpose. These goals cannot be achieved unless there is perseverance and patience as the process can sometimes be challenging and the results slow to attain. A strong volition will assist us to resist distractions and maintain our attention on achieving the goals we have set for ourselves.

- **Action**: We need to systematically pursue the processes that assist us to develop spiritually. We may follow three important processes:

    a) **Nourishment:** Similarly to our body, the soul also needs nourishment to grow and reach its potential. Since the soul is not tangible, the food needed by our soul is not material but spiritual sustenance and energy. Inspiring thoughts and ideas can uplift our soul. This is particularly true of prayer and the study of spiritual writings that are given to humanity by various religions. Such writings are known to have special spiritual energy that connect us with our Source and Creator.

    b) **Education:** The capacities of the soul are revealed through spiritual education. This consists of developing our virtues—such as trustworthiness, love and generosity—and ensuring that our thoughts, words and deeds reflect these virtues. Learning about spiritual principles and following them in our daily life helps us to change ourselves and our relationship with others.

    c) **Application:** We should learn the spiritual principles and practice the virtues until they become part of our attitude and inner life. Our deeds should reflect our lofty thoughts, ideals and principles. We affect the world through our actions because our deeds can influence the perception of the people around us. Our actions can manifest both positive and negative aspects of our beliefs, and affect the world in a constructive or destructive way. Hence it is important to carefully reflect on the consequences before acting, knowing that we can contribute towards an ever-advancing civilization or work against it. In conclusion, our spiritual transformation and its positive influence on the world will become a reality when our acquired knowledge of our spiritual destiny, and our reflection and meditation on it, are translated into action.

16.6 Activities

16.6.1 Double choice questions

For each statement given below, determine whether it is true or false.

		False	True
a)	Inner capacities unfold without any effort as we grow up.	☐	☐
b)	Developing inner capacities requires personal effort and commitment.	☐	☐
c)	We only need to learn how to develop our inner capacities.	☐	☐
d)	We only need a strong volition to cultivate our inner capacities.	☐	☐
e)	We only need to act on our inner capacities to cultivate them.	☐	☐
f)	We need to combine knowledge, volition and action to cultivate our inner capacities.	☐	☐
g)	A strong volition enables us to make a sustained effort to achieve the goals we have set towards cultivating our inner capacities.	☐	☐
h)	Increasing our knowledge of our physical capacities, enables us to achieve a comfortable life.	☐	☐
i)	Increasing our knowledge of our intellectual capacities, enables us to understand how our mind functions.	☐	☐
j)	Increasing our knowledge of our spiritual capacities, enables us to understand our spiritual strengths and weaknesses.	☐	☐
k)	Increasing our knowledge of our spiritual capacities, enables us to be aware of the spiritual qualities of the people around us.	☐	☐
l)	Actions to cultivate our inner capacities consist of nourishment and education.	☐	☐

m) Actions to cultivate our inner capacities consist of nourishment, education and application. ☐ ☐

n) The inner capacities of our soul are nourished through positive and inspiring thoughts. ☐ ☐

o) The inner capacities of our mind are nourished through good diet and exercise. ☐ ☐

p) The inner capacities of our body are nourished by eating to excess. ☐ ☐

q) Spiritual transformation and real change will occur when our reflection and meditation on our acquired knowledge about our spiritual destiny are translated into deeds. ☐ ☐

16.6.2 Short answer questions

1. What is the "knowledge" stage in the unveiling of inner capacities strategy?

   _____
   _____
   _____
   _____

2. What is the "volition" stage in the unveiling of inner capacities strategy?

   _____
   _____
   _____
   _____

3. What is the "action" stage in the unveiling of inner capacities strategy?

   _____
   _____

4. How does the strategy of knowledge, volition and action assist us in realizing our inner capacities? Give an example.

5. Describe the steps involved in realizing our physical capacities using the knowledge, volition and action strategy.

6. Describe the steps involved in realizing our intellectual capacities using the knowledge, volition and action strategy.

7. Describe the steps involved in realizing our spiritual capacities using the knowledge, volition and action strategy.

8. How can we nurture our soul and its inner capacities?

9. What is spiritual transformation?

10. Reflect on the following stories. Determine whether the desires and aspirations expressed by the individuals develop their physical capacities, intellectual capacities or spiritual capacities?

    a) Annette's ambition in life is to be a nurse. She loves to help people. This will enable her to help those who really need help.

    b) John believes that life is about having a good time and enjoying the best of everything that life offers. He would work hard to earn sufficient money to afford such a life style.

    c) Adam's ambition in life is to be a teacher. He likes the job because it provides him with the opportunity to educate the next generation. This will be a great contribution to society.

d) Jasmine is determined to realize her full potential and to excel in everything. Her struggle is not a competition against others but against her own self.

16.6.3 Project

Develop a personal plan for cultivating your spiritual capacities by following the knowledge, volition and action strategy. Devise your plan according to the following steps:

a) Identify the knowledge you have to acquire.
b) Identify how you can develop a strong motivation and volition.
c) Identify how you are you going to nurture your soul.
d) Identify how you are going to cultivate your inner capacities.
e) Identify how you are going to sustain your spiritual growth.

17 Education

17.1 Introduction

As highlighted in previous chapters, the primary purpose of physical life is to cultivate and unfold the capacities hidden in our realities. The capacities developed should be deployed towards advancement of two major processes: the spiritual development of the individual and advancement of human material and spiritual civilization. With such a lofty aim, the development of the inner capacities should not be left to chance. The focus of this chapter is on the role of education in the process of cultivating the inner gifts. We need three different types of education: physical, intellectual and spiritual to unfold our physical, intellectual and spiritual capacities. Despite their differences, these three types of education play complementary roles in effectively realizing the primary purpose of physical life—the spiritual development of an individual.

In this chapter, you need to reflect on and understand the following key points:

a) The inner capacities inherent in human realities can be effectively cultivated and unfolded through education and training.
b) We require physical, intellectual and spiritual education to respectively unveil our physical, intellectual and spiritual capacities.
c) Physical education and training is concerned with the development and well-being of the human body, encouraging a healthier and more enjoyable lifestyle.

d) The primary aim of intellectual education is to cultivate the intellectual capacities and abilities within our intellectual reality.
e) Spiritual education is concerned with the development of the capacities and qualities inherent in the human soul.
f) The three types of education play complementary roles in effectively realizing the spiritual development of an individual.

17.2 Education and inner capacities

As highlighted in the previous chapter, the primary purpose of the physical life is to cultivate and unfold the capacities hidden in our human reality. The developed capacities should be deployed towards advancement of two major processes: the spiritual development of the individual and advancement of the human material and spiritual civilization. With such a lofty aim, the development of the inner capacities cannot be left to chance.

Since the inception of civilization, humanity has been conscious that every individual has potential to acquire attitudes, knowledge, understanding and skills through systematic training and education. Hence, the discipline of education has developed as a means for developing the character, mind and physical abilities of the human.

The word education is derived from the Latin word *educare* which means "to bring up" and related to the word *educere* meaning "to bring forth what is within", and "to bring out potential". Humans can be considered as a mine full of invaluable gems. Through education, these treasures can be uncovered and developed to benefit humanity.[1] These gems are the innate gifts embedded in the human physical, intellectual and spiritual realities as discussed in the previous chapters.

The contributions made by creative, talented and hardworking individuals to human civilization is reflected in the art, music and literature of every generation; has been recorded in books of science and mathematics; and has now also been collected and stored in the electronic media. Another significant role of education is to transfer this accumulated knowledge, and the skills and values from one generation to the next.

---

[1] Baha'u'llah, *Gleanings from the Writings of Bahá'u'lláh*, p. 260.

The methods and approaches used to cultivate the capacities within each reality are unique and different. Hence, it is possible to identify three broad categories of education corresponding to the three realities of man; physical education, intellectual education, and spiritual education.

17.2.1 Physical education

Physical education is concerned with the development and well-being of the human body, and encouraging a healthier and more enjoyable lifestyle through regular physical exercise. In many schools around the world, physical education is an important element of the overall curriculum. The primary aim of physical education is to motivate students to participate in activities that increase physical fitness: sports, health and drug education, gymnastics and some aspects of dance.

An interesting comparison can be made between the physical education of children and animals, sharing as they do the commonality of a physical reality. In the wild, animals learn through imitating their parents; and their development of fitness, strength and agility is totally instinctive. Although some wild animals can be domesticated through appropriate training and education, this is done by harnessing their instincts. For example, animals that live in herds or packs learn to accept man as the "leader of the pack" or the "top of the pecking order"—i.e. the one who must be obeyed. There are some animals, especially among the big carnivores, that are quite unsuitable for domestication other than in exceptional circumstances. Others, such as dogs and cats, have been domesticated for countless generations, having discovered for themselves the advantages of the warmth and food scraps available around the campfires of primitive man.

Animals can be trained to perform specific tasks such as pulling a plough or wagon. For some animals, such as racehorses, their training is specifically designed to bring them to their fullest potential of speed and endurance. It is instinctive behaviour for a horse to run from its predators and, when it strives to win a race, it is due to its innate desire to seek safety at the front of the herd. The touch of a jockey's whip merely reminds the racehorse of the predator's claws.

The inborn loyalty of some canine species makes them excellent as guide-dogs and companions for the visually impaired, while the sense of smell of others can be utilized for many purposes such as to trail a criminal, or to sniff out drugs or explosives.

However, despite the level of proficiency that animals can achieve when they have been selectively trained for a task that makes use of their instincts, they have no idea about the purpose of their physical training other than the reward they have learned to expect from man. In comparison, even young children can understand the purpose of physical education, and learn to enjoy sport for its own sake as well as for the sense of achievement that excellence brings.

17.2.2 Intellectual education

In previous chapters, we have highlighted that human civilization is created and advanced as the result of the intellectual contributions made by the individuals of a society. The primary aim of intellectual education is to cultivate the intellectual capacities and abilities within the intellectual reality of every individual. This is achieved by developing the general powers of the mind. This type of education is exclusive to man, since animals do not have an intellectual reality.

We also previously mentioned that the mind emerges through the interaction of the mental powers of the soul, the human spirit and the processing power of the human brain. The general powers of the mind include the four mental powers of imagination, thought, understanding and memory—emanating from the soul, and the power of reasoning.

Intellectual education involves two stages: the development and enhancement of our four mental powers and the power of reasoning; and the application of them to a field of human endeavour and civilization building.

For example, the power of thought can be made more effective by learning to think critically and systematically. Studying mathematics, language and logic can help us to become more efficient and convincing in our reasoning. In the second process, we apply our mental powers to master a particular field of human endeavour and civilization building. For example, through the study of physics, mathematics and various technologies, we can become civil engineers, responsible for the design and construction of our cities, and the maintenance of their infrastructure and the transport networks that connect them.

Hence, intellectual education is the driving force behind the development of civilization as it creates and advances government, administration, medical services, education, charitable works, trades, arts and handicrafts, sciences, great inventions and discoveries, and complex institutions.

17.2.3 Spiritual education

Spiritual education is concerned with the development of the capacities and qualities inherent in the human soul. Since the dawn of human civilization, the cultivation of human spiritual qualities has always been of great interest to religious scholars, educators and parents.

Spiritual education fosters the realization of the spiritual potential and the development of the spiritual capacities in an individual. This ensures the emergence of a strong spiritual-self that can effectively encourage and empower the ego to transcend self-interest and transform the attitudes and behaviour of the individual.

Hence, through spiritual education, virtues become manifested in human attitudes, words and deeds. This brings about true happiness and peace for individuals and for the people around them.

There is no doubt that the spiritual education of the individual will result in the transformation of the society and collective spiritual growth of humanity.

17.3 Primary purpose of education

The primary purpose of physical life for every individual is to develop his innate spiritual gifts and capacities. This is achieved through the collective operation and interaction of the three realities of the human. This highlights the importance of spiritual education as the most critical and essential element in any educational program aimed at cultivating the inner gifts of an individual.

However, this does not mean that physical and intellectual education can be ignored. The physical body is the primary means and instrument for living in the material world. As such, it is important that the body is sound and functions efficiently. The mind of man is the key in making critical and moral decisions in everyday life. An individual can contribute more effectively to the progress of civilization when his/her intellectual capacities are well cultivated.

Hence, all three types of education are essential to empower and enable an individual to fulfil his purpose in life. However, these different components of training should play complementary roles to effectively realize the spiritual development of the individual. Otherwise, spiritual progress, the main purpose of the physical life of an individual, is not realized.

17.4 Activities

17.4.1 Double choice questions

For each statement given below, determine whether it is true or false.

		False	True
a)	Education will only cultivate the hidden gifts in our physical reality.	☐	☐
b)	Education will only cultivate the hidden gifts in our intellectual reality.	☐	☐
c)	Education will only cultivate the hidden gifts in our spiritual reality.	☐	☐
d)	Education will cultivate the hidden gifts in all three realities.	☐	☐
e)	Physical education is concerned with the development and well-being of the human body.	☐	☐
f)	Physical education is exclusive to man.	☐	☐
g)	Intellectual education is exclusive to man.	☐	☐
h)	Spiritual education is exclusive to man.	☐	☐
i)	The aim of intellectual education is to cultivate the intellectual capacities within every individual.	☐	☐
j)	Human civilization is the result of physical education.	☐	☐
k)	Intellectual education is concerned with the development of the capacities inherent in the human soul.	☐	☐
l)	Spiritual education fosters the realization of the spiritual potential and the development of the spiritual capacities in an individual.	☐	☐

m) Spiritual education is concerned with the development of the capacities and qualities inherent in the human soul. ☐ ☐

n) The powers of the mind are enhanced by spiritual education. ☐ ☐

o) Spiritual education is the most critical and essential element in any educational program aimed at cultivating the inner gifts of an individual. ☐ ☐

p) Spiritual education is so important that physical and intellectual education can be ignored. ☐ ☐

q) All three types of education are essential to empower and enable an individual to fulfil his purpose in life. ☐ ☐

17.4.2 Short answer questions

1. What is the meaning of the word "education" and what is its Latin root?

   _____
   _____
   _____
   _____

2. How does education help the individual?

   _____
   _____
   _____
   _____

3. What type of education and training do you need if you desire to improve your stamina? Explain.

   _____
   _____

4. What type of education do you need if you desire to improve your ability to develop convincing arguments? Explain.

5. What type of education do you need if you desire to acquire virtues? Explain.

6. What should be the ultimate purpose of education? Explain.

7. Is it possible to enhance the mental powers of the mind? Give an example.

8. Why are all three types of education important for the spiritual growth of an individual?

_____
_____
_____

9. How can the three types of education complement each other?
_____
_____
_____
_____

10. Reflect on the following stories. Determine what type of education, physical, intellectual or spiritual, or a combination of them, can assist each individual to achieve his/her desires and aspirations?

   a) Annette's ambition in life is to be a nurse. She loves to help people. This will enable her to help those who really need help.
   _____
   _____
   _____
   _____

   b) John believes that life is about having a good time and enjoying the best of everything that life offers. He would work hard to earn sufficient money to afford such a life style.
   _____
   _____
   _____
   _____

   c) Adam's ambition in life is to be a teacher. He likes the job and also it provides him with the opportunity to educate the next generation. He believes this will be a great contribution to his society.
   _____
   _____
   _____

d) Jasmine is determined to realize her full potential and to excel in everything. Her struggle is not a competition against others but against her own self.

_____
_____
_____
_____

17.4.3 Project

Devise a personal plan for developing your inner capacities and gifts during the next 12 months. Your plan should include the following steps:

a) Identify one or more specific goals that would develop your physical capacities.
b) Identify one or more specific goals that would develop your intellectual capacities.
c) Identify one or more specific goals that would develop your spiritual capacities.
d) For each goal you have defined in (a) to (c) identify what specific actions (education and training) you are going to undertake to achieve the goal.

18 RELIGION

18.1 Introduction

In the previous chapters we looked at the roles of personal endeavour and education in cultivating our inner capacities. However, no study can ignore the overall influence that religion has had, whether directly or indirectly, on the individual and on human society. Religion has proved to be a powerful force in unfolding human inner gifts. The impact of religion is not only on our thoughts and attitudes but on our actions and deeds. Archaeological discoveries indicate that human religious experience is as old as humanity. Pre-historic humans believed in life after death as far back as 150,000 years ago. It is impossible to deny the existence of religion and its intrinsic role in the progress of human civilization. Over the course of history, there have been conflicting views on the nature and origin of religion. It is possible to identify two major categories for these views: materialistic and spiritual.

In this chapter, you need to reflect on and understand the following key points:

a) Archaeological discoveries indicate that human religious experience is as old as humanity.
b) Founders of the main world religions have usually been special individuals who are referred to by such terms as Prophets, Messengers of God or Manifestations of God, etc.
c) A Manifestation of God claims to have a mission from God to educate humanity and advance human civilization.
d) Materialistic views of religion dispute the spiritual nature of religion and its divine origin.

e) Materialistic views fail to explain some fundamental questions about the birth, development and influence of religion on the progress of human civilization.
f) From a spiritual point of view, religion is divinely inspired. It means that one special individual, known as the Manifestation of God, is chosen by God to act as His mouthpiece and to give His message to humanity.
g) The Manifestations of God can be considered as the true educators of humanity.

18.2 Definition of religion

The word "religion" is defined as a socially organized collection of beliefs, cultural values and world views that have a respect for the sacred, reverence for God (or the gods), and is an expression of the bond between man and God. It is derived from the Latin word *religio*. Archaeological discoveries indicate that human religious experience is as old as humanity. Such evidences demonstrate that pre-historic humans believed in life after death as far back as 150,000 years ago. Remains of early examples of art and architecture reflect human piety and religious experiences more explicitly from around five thousand years ago.

Founders of religion have usually been special individuals who are referred to by various terms such as Prophet, Messenger of God or Manifestation of God. A Manifestation of God is divinely inspired by God and entrusted with a mission from God to educate humanity and advance human civilization.

A study of past religions shows that the Manifestations of God have very similar characteristics and patterns of development. Each appears among a group of people who are in need of spiritual, and sometimes material, renewal and development. He provides them with a set of teachings and spiritual principles to nurture and empower them to realize the purpose of their lives, and contribute towards the emergence of a materially and spiritually prosperous society.

Humans have always been aware of their spiritual reality. They have felt that the world of existence has a depth beyond the physical reality. Experiencing and understanding this transcendent and spiritual reality requires more than the five senses through which man perceives the physical world. Religion has always responded to man's need for transcendence by offering an environment in which man can experience spirituality and receive the spiritual nourishment required to cultivate and enhance spiritual qualities.

Hence, it is impossible to deny the existence of religion and its intrinsic role in the progress of human civilization. However, there have been conflicting views on the nature and origin of religion, particularly in modern times. It is possible to identify two major categories for these views: materialistic and spiritual.

18.3 Materialistic view on the nature of religion

The materialistic view of religion, originating from the materialistic view of human nature, has a long history that goes back more than 2,000 years to the time of the Roman Empire. In the previous chapters, it was indicated that the human spiritual reality is denied by the materialistic view. The human spiritual, emotional and intellectual characteristics are claimed to be the product of the human physical reality.

Similarly, the materialistic view of religion contests the spiritual nature of religion and its divine origin. Primarily, it suggests that religion is the creation of the human mind to explain the unknown and to satisfy the biological, social and political needs of man.

In addition to this core materialistic assumption, various philosophers have also criticised the concepts and practices of religions based on their personal experience of a particular religion, and observations of the religions as practiced in their society.

For example, Karl Marx (5 May 1818—14 March 1883), a German philosopher who disagreed with the capitalist economic system, considered religion as a tool used by the ruling class to exploit the masses. By promising eventual happiness in the life to come, religion discourages the masses from making any sustained effort to identify, understand and overcome the real source of their suffering, which in Marx's opinion was capitalism. He refers to religion as the opium of the people. Marx also criticised the Christian doctrine of original sin as anti-social, convincing people that the source of their misery was inherent in the unchangeable sinfulness of humanity.

As another example, Sam Harris (born April 9, 1967), a contemporary atheist, suggests that the time has come to unreservedly question the idea of religious faith, otherwise, the survival of human civilization will be endangered. He criticizes Judaism, Christianity and Islám as being so uncompromising that fanatical followers are ready to harm themselves and others for the sake of their religion.

A careful analysis of such views shows that they are narrow and subjective and largely target the man-made practices and superstitions that have crept into various religions over the centuries, rather than the original message and teachings revealed by the Manifestations of God.

The materialistic view also fails to explain some fundamental questions about the birth and development of a religion, and its influence on the progress of human civilization.

Although, the majority of the Manifestations of God were uneducated, They exhibited innate knowledge. Their teachings were extremely progressive for the time and resulted in the emergence of advanced civilizations. This cannot be explained by scientific laws and could only be possible through a power beyond the physical world.

In nearly all religions, the majority of the followers accept the message only after the physical life of the Founder has ended. How can an individual without any earthly power and political influence attract millions of people to follow his teachings after his death? This also cannot be scientifically explained.

18.4 Spiritual view on the nature of religion

A spiritual point of view believes religion is divinely inspired. According to this view, an individual, known as the Manifestation of God, is chosen by God to act as His mouthpiece and to give His message to humanity. Each new Manifestation of God renews the fundamental reality of religion and reveals another aspect of the absolute truth previously hidden from humanity, but appropriate for that particular age. Hence, the teachings and writings of a Manifestation of God are referred to as "revelation".

The purpose of religion is to safeguard the interests of humanity and to create peace and unity amongst them, although humanity has often used religion as an excuse to wage war. Peace and unity is achieved through the spiritual education of the individual and a collective transformation of the society. The writings and teachings in a religion play a critical role in this process. Bahá'u'lláh states: *"The Purpose of the one true God, exalted be His glory, in revealing Himself unto men is to lay bare those gems that lie hidden within the mine of their true and inmost selves."*[1]

In another statement, Bahá'u'lláh further describes the purpose of God in sending His Prophets:

"Every Prophet Whom the Almighty and Peerless Creator hath purposed to send to the peoples of the earth hath been entrusted with a Message, and charged to act in a manner that would best meet the requirements of the age in which He appeared. God's purpose in sending His Prophets unto men is twofold. The first is to liberate the children of men from the darkness of ignorance, and guide them to the light of true understanding. The second is to ensure the peace and tranquillity of mankind, and provide all the means by which they can be established."[2]

Although the scope of every religion is broad, and many issues and topics are addressed, the content of revelation fits into one of the following categories:

- **Sacred writings and prayers**: These provide spiritual nourishment for the human soul and are intended to assist in the cultivation of spiritual capacities.
- **Personal laws**: These are intended to guide and empower the believers to develop and maintain a healthy and spiritual lifestyle.
- **Social teachings**: The revelation of a religion is a response to the social challenges faced by humanity. The social teachings of a revelation provide guidance for humanity to overcome those challenges and to further advance civilization.

18.5 True Educators

As explained in the previous chapters, humanity is in need of physical, intellectual and spiritual education. Human material civilization has developed effective methods to provide physical and intellectual education.

---

[1] Bahá'u'lláh, *Gleanings from the Writings of Bahá'u'lláh*, p. 156.
[2] Bahá'u'lláh, *Gleanings from the Writings of Bahá'u'lláh*, p. 79.

Spiritual education can be obtained only through religion. Bahá'u'lláh describes the education of humanity as the only purpose of religion: *"The Prophets and Messengers of God have been sent down for the sole purpose of guiding mankind to the straight Path of Truth. The purpose underlying Their revelation hath been to educate all men ..."*[1]

Religion also provides guidance and direction for the physical and intellectual development of an individual and a society. Hence, the Manifestations of God can be considered as the True Educators of humanity.

In every age, the teachings revealed by the Manifestation of God provide humanity with an education that harmonizes material, intellectual and spiritual development.

For example, Moses as a true Educator of humanity, arose in order to rescue the children of Israel when they were in the lowest degree of ignorance and heedlessness and lived under the bonds of slavery. As Moses led the children of Israel to the Holy Land, He educated them physically, intellectually and spiritually. His followers acquired worth and honour, excelled in civilization and were enabled to establish the great Kingdom of Solomon. Moses achieved all these victories through divine power not earthly power or riches.

Similarly, Christ single-handedly established great divine standards and teachings that have transformed the lives of individuals and influenced great nations such as the Romans, Greeks, Egyptian, Syrians and others. His teachings brought about peace and justice among people who had previously been inimical and alienated.

Muḥammad appeared among Arabs who lived in the utmost state of degradation and barbarism to the extent that fathers often buried their baby daughters alive. The Arabs were split up into various hostile and warring tribes. Muḥammad educated and unified these people and enabled them to establish a great civilization, spreading into Africa, India and Europe and carrying with them significant advances in science and governance as well as in moral standards.

---

[1] Bahá'u'lláh, *Gleanings from the Writings of Bahá'u'lláh*, p. 156.

18.6 Activities

18.6.1 Double choice questions

For each statement given below, determine whether it is true or false.

		False	True
a)	Religion is a recent phenomenon in human history.	☐	☐
b)	Human religious experience is as old as humanity.	☐	☐
c)	Arts and architecture began to reflect human piety and religious experience from around twenty thousand years ago.	☐	☐
d)	Religion offers an environment within which to experience spirituality and to receive spiritual nourishment.	☐	☐
e)	The materialistic view of religion has developed in modern times.	☐	☐
f)	The materialistic view of religion contests the spiritual nature of religion and its divine origin.	☐	☐
g)	The materialistic view of religion suggests that religion is the creation of science to explain the unknown and to fulfil biological, social and political needs.	☐	☐
h)	The criticisms made against religion have been subjective, and largely target the man-made practices and superstitions that have crept into religion, rather than the original teachings revealed by the Founder.	☐	☐
i)	The majority of the Manifestations of God were educated.	☐	☐
j)	The Manifestations of God established their religion through divine power.	☐	☐
k)	The spiritual point of view claims that religion is divinely inspired.	☐	☐

l) The main purpose of religion is to educate and develop the intellectual reality of man. ☐ ☐

m) Prayers and inspirational writings are the main part of the teachings revealed by a Manifestation of God. ☐ ☐

n) Personal laws are the main part of the teachings revealed by a Manifestation of God. ☐ ☐

o) Social teachings are the main part of the teachings revealed by a Manifestation of God. ☐ ☐

p) The content of revelation consist of prayers and inspirational writings, personal laws and social teachings. ☐ ☐

q) The Manifestations of God are the true educators of humanity. ☐ ☐

18.6.2 Short answer questions

1. What is the meaning of the word "religion"?

_____
_____
_____
_____

2. How old is human religious experience?

_____
_____
_____
_____

3. Why has religion appealed to the majority of humanity?

_____
_____
_____

4. Who are the Manifestations of God?

5. What is the purpose of religion?

6. What is revelation?

7. What are the assumptions behind the materialistic view of religion?

8. What are the main drawbacks of the materialistic view of religion?

9. Give two examples of how the birth and development of a religion cannot be explained by scientific laws.

   _____
   _____
   _____
   _____

10. What are the assumptions behind the spiritual view of religion?

    _____
    _____
    _____
    _____

11. What does the revelation of a religion consist of?

    _____
    _____
    _____
    _____

12. Why are the Manifestations of God called the True Educators of humanity?

    _____
    _____
    _____
    _____

13. Consider the following story about Jesus Christ, the Manifestation of God in Christianity:

    Christians are the followers of Jesus Christ who was born in Bethlehem, Judea, between 6 and 4 BC. He grew up in Nazareth, Galilee. At the age of about 30, He was baptized in the Jordan River by a prophet called John the Baptist. John had been preaching and baptizing people as a mark of repentance for their sins. He heralded the coming of one greater than himself.

After his baptism, Jesus gathered around him 12 disciples and travelled around Palestine preaching, teaching, and healing and restoring life. He announced the coming of God's rule on earth and declared the need for people to repent of their sins. Peter, the leader of the disciples declared Him as the Messiah of the Jewish people.[1] At the age of about thirty three, Jesus was arrested, tortured and crucified on a cross. Hence, Jesus lived only for three years after His declaration as the Messiah. Despite the short time, His message still influences the hearts of people. There are currently around two billion Christians in the world who follow His teachings.

a) Do you observe anything extraordinary about this story?

_____
_____
_____
_____

b) How could Jesus have achieved such a sovereignty after His death and have continued to attract the hearts of so many people over the past two thousand years?

_____
_____
_____
_____

18.6.3 Project

Here are some major religions that have emerged over the last 6,000 years, since the beginning of written history:

- Hinduism
- Judaism
- Zoroastrianism
- Buddhism

---

[1] Luke 9:20

- Christianity
- Islám
- The Bahá'í Faith

Choose one of these religions and conduct the following research on it.

a) Where was the birthplace of the religion?
b) Which Manifestation of God founded that religion?
c) What was His background?
d) How old is the religion?
e) How many people follow this religion?
f) Find two examples of inspirational writing and prayers of the religion.
g) Identify two personal laws prescribed by the religion.
h) Identify two social teachings introduced by the religion?

19 Four Seasons of a Religion

19.1 Introduction

In spite the spiritual nature of religion, the laws and processes under which a religion is born and developed have counterparts in the physical world. Natural events in the physical world pass through cycles. A religion also evolves and develops through the cycles of spiritual birth and decay during its lifetime. The cycle of birth, growth, maturity and decay of a religion has close similarities to the four seasons of a year. We refer to it as the spiritual cycle of religion. The resemblance of the four seasons of the year and the spiritual cycle of religion is explored in this chapter. This will shed more light on the nature of religion.

In this chapter, you need to reflect on and understand the following key points:

a) The physical world is a counterpart of the spiritual world.
b) The cycle of birth, growth, maturity and decay of a religion is analogous to the four seasons of a year.
c) The birth of a new religion represents the spring of the spiritual cycle since the appearance of a new religion releases fresh spiritual energies throughout the world.
d) The spiritual summer represents the stage of strength and maturity of a religion.
e) With the arrival of the spiritual autumn, the spiritual influence, purity and sacredness of the religion diminishes.
f) The winter of the spiritual cycle is marked by the darkness of human error and ignorance about human spiritual reality.

g) When the winter of religion has completed its course, a new religion is born and another spiritual springtime begins.
h) The Manifestations of God are in perfect unity and the religions brought by them are one although they are revealed at different times in stages appropriate to the varying levels of human development.

19.2 Physical world a counterpart of spiritual world

The spiritual reality of man and the soul are strong evidences for the existence of a spiritual world beyond the physical world that we perceive through our five senses. Although the nature and the reality of the physical and spiritual worlds are different; they are counterparts of each other in that they are governed by comparable processes and functions specific to each world.

The development of the inner spiritual capacities of man is an example of such a correspondence. Although the nature of these capacities in the physical and spiritual realities of man is different, similar laws apply to both. For example, as with man's physical reality, cultivating the inner spiritual capacities requires personal effort, education and nourishment. If these capacities are not nurtured, no growth will occur. Although the nature of the nourishment, education and growth are different in the physical and spiritual worlds, they are both regulated by similar laws.[1]

19.3 Spiritual cycle of religion

Religion has a spiritual origin and, therefore, belongs to the spiritual world. However, the laws and processes under which a religion is born and developed have counterparts in the physical world.

In the physical world, natural events pass through cycles. For example, time evolves through a continuous cycle of days, nights, months and years. Each year consists of four seasons.

A study of past major religions shows that each has evolved and developed through the cycles of spiritual birth, maturity and decay in its lifetime. The cycle of birth, growth, maturity and decay of a

---

[1] 'Abdu'l-Bahá, *Tablet of the Universe.*

religion is analogous to the four seasons of the year. We refer to it as the spiritual cycle of religion.

In the following sections, we explore the similarities between the four seasons of the year and the spiritual cycle of religion.

19.3.1 Spiritual springtime

The birth of a new religion represents the springtime of the spiritual cycle. In the physical world, the arrival of the spring season regenerates life and restores vigour to all living things. The fresh breeze, showers of rain and warming sun revitalise plants and animals alike. Vegetation grows new branches, leaves and blossoms. The fragrance of flowers fills the air. People feel charged with new energy and vitality. Hence, the physical spring is the source of new life and spirit.

Similarly, the appearance of a new religion releases fresh spiritual energies throughout the world. This energy gives a new life to the reality of man. Those who directly receive this energy become spiritually transformed, manifesting remarkable capacities and achievements.

The released spiritual forces initiate new spiritual processes that lead to fundamental changes within the society in which the religion has appeared, and advances its affairs.

19.3.2 Summer of achievement

With the coming of the physical summer, the air and the earth warm up, and growth and development in the vegetable kingdom accelerates towards maturity. Fruit appears on the trees, and grain crops develop their seed heads, giving a glimpse of a coming time of plenty. The processes that were initiated in nature during springtime reach their stage of perfection and produce outcomes. By the end of summer the crops are ready for harvesting.

The spiritual summer represents the stage of strength and maturity of a religion. The spiritual forces released in the springtime have worked through the human reality and cultivated their inner capacities. The result is the spiritual transformation of the individual and the collective transformation of society. The teachings and laws of the religion are well established and have created an environment conducive to the holistic and sustainable development of agriculture, commerce and industry. The religion produces its perfect outcomes during its spiritual summer.

19.3.3 Turbulent autumn

At the end of the fullness of the physical summer, autumn arrives—the main harvest season when the fruits of summer are collected and stored. Farmers hurry to bring in the harvest before the appearance of autumnal storms. Now wild unwholesome winds start to gust and blow, and temperatures begin to drop. Vegetation loses its vigour and vitality. Leaves on trees turn yellow and fall to the ground. Flowers disappear from gardens. In the world of nature, this is the time of death and decay.

With the arrival of the spiritual autumn, the spiritual influence of the religion diminishes, and purity and sacredness wanes. The vitality of the religion declines until only its rituals and manmade forms remain. Superstitions, misconceptions and illusions overshadow the reality of the religion. Divisions appear among the followers and the integrity of their faith is lost. All the above signs indicate the decline and degeneration of the religion.

19.3.4 Winter of despondency

With the coming of winter, nature is gripped by storms and freezing cold. Days become darker and shorter. The soil appears barren as perennial plants become dormant, and trees stand exposed with their starkly naked branches burdened with hoar frost and overhung with icicles. With the disappearance of edible vegetation, many animals go into hibernation in order to survive the lack of food and the bitter cold.

Similarly, the winter of the spiritual cycle is marked by the darkness of human error and ignorance regarding the human spiritual reality. Indifference, disobedience, disunity and strife dominate the relationships between people and their societies. Oppression and injustice become rampant. As goodness declines, humanity suffers.

The winter of a religion weakens the foundations of morality and spirituality within a society. People become disillusioned, apathetic and confused, and are unable to recognize the truth. However, the extreme decadence and corruption drives some individuals to start searching for a solution. At this stage, when the winter of religion has completed its course, a new religion is born and another spiritual springtime begins.

19.4 Concept of progressive revelation

The spiritual cycle of a religion explains why there are so many religions in the world today. In the past, every religion was revealed at a particular time for a specific people in response to their physical, intellectual and spiritual needs. Hence, the religious truth that they received relates to a specific time and location.

A new religion arrives whenever a society is inflicted by complex social problems and the people are weakened in their spiritual beliefs. God appoints a divine Educator from among the people. This Educator breathes a new spiritual life into the society and gives them guidance on how to deal with their social problems.

The concept of the renewal of religion is known in the Bahá'í Faith as "progressive revelation". Humanity is not able to achieve the purpose of its physical life without assistance. Hence, God has progressively sent His Manifestations to guide and assist humanity. Over the course of human history, the Manifestations of God have helped individuals to grow spiritually and have provided the necessary teachings and laws to overcome the social and economic problems emerging in human society. As a result, humanity has collectively evolved and continues to grow from one stage of development to the next towards its final destiny.

The Manifestations of God are like clear mirrors that perfectly reflect the true image and attributes of God. Hence, They are in perfect unity with each other, and the apparently different religions brought by them are, in reality, one and the same, though revealing different aspects or levels of that same truth according to the capacities of the peoples at different stages of human development. The unity of religions is explained by 'Abdu'l-Bahá in the following statement:

> *"In the Word of God there is still another unity—the oneness of the Manifestations of God, Abraham, Moses, Jesus Christ, Muḥammad, the Báb and Bahá'u'lláh. This is a unity divine, heavenly, radiant, merciful—the one reality appearing in its successive Manifestations. For instance, the sun is one and the same, but its points of dawning are various. During the*

summer season it rises from the northern point of the ecliptic; in winter it appears from the southern point of rising. Each month between, it appears from a certain zodiacal position. Although these dawning points are different, the sun is the same sun, which has appeared from them all. The significance is the reality of Prophethood which is symbolized by the sun, and the holy Manifestations are the dawning places or zodiacal points."[1]

---

[1] 'Abdu'l-Bahá, *The Promulgation of Universal Peace*, p. 192.

19.5 Activities

19.5.1 Double choice questions

For each statement given below, determine whether it is true or false.

		False	True
a)	The physical and spiritual worlds are counterparts to each other.	☐	☐
b)	The nature of the physical and the spiritual worlds is similar.	☐	☐
c)	There are analogous processes and functions operating in the physical and the spiritual worlds.	☐	☐
d)	The origin of religion is in the physical world.	☐	☐
e)	The cycle of birth, growth, maturity and decay of a religion has similarities to the four seasons of the year.	☐	☐
f)	The spiritual summer represents the stage of strength and maturity of a religion.	☐	☐
g)	The spiritual summer is the final stage in the development of a religion.	☐	☐
h)	The spiritual springtime of a religion is the most quiet and slow stage in the development of a new religion.	☐	☐
i)	The appearance of a new religion releases fresh spiritual energies throughout the world.	☐	☐
j)	A religion produces its perfect outcomes during its spiritual summer.	☐	☐
k)	With the arrival of the spiritual autumn, the spiritual influence of the religion significantly increases.	☐	☐
l)	With the arrival of the spiritual autumn, the vitality of religion fades, and only rituals and forms remain.	☐	☐
m)	The winter of the spiritual cycle is marked	☐	☐

      by the darkness of human error and ignorance about the human spiritual reality.

n) Indifference, disobedience, disunity and strife dominate the people and their relationships with each other during the spiritual autumn. ☐ ☐

o) When the winter of religion has completed its course, a new religion is born and another spiritual springtime starts. ☐ ☐

p) During the spiritual summer, the spiritual qualities of the believers weaken and are replaced by vices such as self-love, selfishness and greed. ☐ ☐

q) During the winter of a religion, people are disillusioned and confused, and fail to see the truth. ☐ ☐

r) The Manifestations of God are fundamentally different from each other. ☐ ☐

s) The Manifestations of God are like perfect mirrors reflecting the attributes of God. ☐ ☐

19.5.2 Short answer questions

1. Is the origin of religion in the physical world or spiritual world? Explain.

   _____
   _____
   _____
   _____

2. What is your understanding of the statement: "The physical and spiritual worlds are counterparts of each other"?

   _____
   _____
   _____
   _____

3. What is a cycle?

___

4. Identify some cycles in the physical world.

___

5. What is the spiritual cycle of a religion?

___

6. What are the effects of the spiritual forces released by a new religion?

___

7. What are the main characteristics of the springtime of a religion?

___

8. What are the main characteristics of the summer of a religion?

9. What are the main characteristics of the autumn of a religion?

10. What are the main characteristics of the winter of a religion?

11. What happens when the winter of a religion is completed?

12. Spiritually, which season of a religion is worse; autumn or spring? Why?

13. How long is the spiritual cycle of a religion?

_____
_____
_____
_____

14. Describe your understanding of the oneness of the Manifestations of God.

_____
_____
_____
_____

15. What is the concept of progressive revelation?

_____
_____
_____
_____

16. Consider the following criticisms made against religion. Using the concept of the four seasons of religion, develop an argument to illustrate that the criticism is a misunderstanding of the nature of religion. You can draw on characteristics defined for the autumn and winter of religion in the chapter.

    a) Religious beliefs are primarily superstitions and manmade illusions.

    _____
    _____
    _____
    _____

    b) Religions are without spirit and consist only of forms and rituals.

    _____
    _____

c) Religions are the cause of war and conflict, rather than love and unity.

d) Religious people are as selfish and greedy as non-believers.

e) Religion cannot spiritually uplift people and assist with their spiritual development.

f) Religion cannot provide solutions for the problems faced by the society today.

19.5.3 Project

Here are some major religions that have emerged over the last 6,000 years, since the beginning of written history:

- Hinduism
- Judaism
- Zoroastrianism
- Buddhism
- Christianity
- Islám
- The Bahá'í Faith

Choose one the above religions and conduct the research described below:

a) Write a summary of the history and development of the religion.
b) Identify the four seasons of the religion and the characteristics of each season.
c) Do the identified seasons match the description provided for them in this lesson?

Section IV – A mystical journey

20 GOD, THE CREATOR

20.1 Introduction

Our study of the universe, life and human nature, so far, clearly shows that the world of existence is complex, diverse and purposeful. It functions accurately and in an orderly fashion, submitting to universal laws. While the vegetable and animal kingdoms manifest characteristics beyond the mineral kingdom, they are still subject to universal laws and obey them precisely. Man represents a unique entity in the world of existence. Although his physical reality is subject to the same universal laws, the influence of his intellectual and spiritual realities causes him to manifest characteristics not observed in nature and the lower kingdoms. This is evident from the culture and civilization that have emerged through the cultivation and unfoldment of the capacities hidden in the human soul.

The supporters of the materialistic view suggest that the universe has emerged as a result of chance and random incidents occurring in nature. However, advocates of the spiritual view argue that the order and beauty evident in the universe could not have occurred through chance and accident. There must be a creator referred to as God who has designed and brought into existence the universe and its diverse elements. In this chapter we will put forward a logical argument for the existence of God and learn how we can acquire knowledge of our Creator.

In this chapter, you need to reflect on and understand the following key points:

a) It is logical to assert that a mighty force is driving the process of evolution in the universe towards greater refinement and a higher order.
b) It is irrational to suggest that the source of this force is produced by nature.
c) Such a force cannot have been produced or controlled by a human agency.
d) The only feasible option is that the force must emanate from a creator referred to as God.
e) The Reality of God is absolutely inaccessible to man.
f) Although for us to know the Manifestation of God is to know God, it does not mean we can know the "reality" of God.

20.2 Logical search for Creator

The universe and all its elements from the many galaxies down to the smallest living organisms on earth are continually evolving towards greater refinement and a higher order. For example, we learned in section 1.3 that scientific discoveries suggest the origin of the universe, consisting of galaxies, stars and planets, may have been the result of a tremendous explosion, known as the Big Bang, within a brief instant of time around fifteen billion years ago. From this chaotic process the galaxies, stars and planets have gradually emerged. A much later result of this evolution has been the appearance of life on earth from simple, single celled organisms. Through evolution and refinement of the living matter, more complex organisms, such as plants, animals and man, have emerged.

A basic principle of physics is that a physical system changes when it is driven by a force. A car moves when the engine is turned on and fuel is converted to energy for the mechanical rotation of the wheels. An apple that has become disconnected from the tree falls to the ground because of the force of gravity.

From the aforementioned examples it is logical to assert that a mighty force is driving the process of evolution in the universe towards greater refinement and a higher order. It is also reasonable to assume that this force has a purpose and follows a well-designed plan rather than acting chaotically and randomly.

Regarding the source of the force, it is irrational to suggest that it is produced by nature. This force has created man with characteristics well above the nature of animals in terms of complexity, order and structure. Nature itself is built, fashioned and transformed by this force. Hence, nature cannot be the source of the force.

It is likewise obvious that the force is not produced nor controlled by man, despite his being the most complex and intelligent known entity in the universe. The force that created man must be far superior and more perfect than man. This is analogous to the way that even the most beautiful painting cannot have created itself but must have been the work of an artist who is incomparably superior to his own masterpiece.

The only possible option for the source of the force, which has designed the universe and is driving it to perfection, must be that it emanates from a Creator incomparably more perfect than the universe, and that man is the Creator's most perfect construct. We refer to the source of this force as God.

20.3 Historical roots of belief in God

Belief in God has been an intrinsic characteristic of man throughout his recorded history. Even human burials as old as 50,000 to 30,000 BC show evidences of belief in a supernal being and of life after death. Religions have played a major role in developing these beliefs. As mentioned in section 19.4 regarding progressive revelation, it is through a succession of Messengers that God has guided man to develop a better understanding of his human station and of his Creator. Hence, the awareness and understanding of the nature God has evolved and progressed with the collective intellectual and social development of man.

In the early stages of human development, belief in God was limited by man's immature powers of reasoning and lack of understanding of the physical world. After the passing of the Messenger for the time, His pure but simplified Teachings would gradually have become clouded with human superstitions born of ignorance and sometimes expressed in barbaric rituals. For example, at the lowest ebb of man's spirituality, human sacrifice even replaced the ritual animal sacrifices traditionally performed in appeasement to the individual gods to whom natural phenomena such as lightning, earthquakes, fire and floods were attributed. The belief in various gods can still be observed in older religions that, even today, have many followers. Despite the superstitions that have dominated these religions, the core teachings still retain the belief in a Creator.

The major religions that have emerged over the last six thousand years of the written history have placed a great emphasis on the oneness of God. Hence, they are known as monotheistic religions. The ability to understand the concept of oneness reflects a new stage in human intellectual and spiritual development. Along with this development have been parallel advances in human material civilization, science and technology; and a better understanding of the physical world. Hence, there has been a great reduction in the influence of superstitions in these religions.

Despite the strong influence of the materialistic culture, the majority of people in today's societies have a strong belief in one God as their Creator. However, they refer to Him by different names according to their language and religion. For example, Alláh in Islám and Yahweh in Judaism refer to the same God as the Creator of the universe.

20.4 Nature of God

According to the teachings of the Bahá'í Faith, representing the latest revelation from God, there is only one God whose reality is absolutely inaccessible to humanity. in every age, God appoints an individual to manifest His Will for the physical, intellectual and spiritual progress of humanity and to reflect His attributes and qualities. This is how humanity acquires a knowledge of God (see section 20.5 for more explanation).

According to the Bahá'í teachings, "What is meant by a personal God is a God Who is conscious of His creation, Who has a Mind, a Will, a Purpose, and not, as many scientists and materialists believe, an unconscious and determined force operating in the universe."[1] The Will of God represents His design for the creation that unfolds through orderly processes of evolution in the physical world as well as the collective intellectual and spiritual evolution of humanity.

---

[1] Shoghi Effendi, in *Lights of Guidance*, p. 477.

20.5 Knowledge of God

According to the teachings of the Bahá'í Faith, *"... the knowledge of the Manifestations of God is the knowledge of God, for the bounties, splendours and divine attributes are apparent in Them."*[1] This refers to the fact that for us to know the Manifestation of God is to know God. It does not imply that the Manifestations of God are the same as God or that They can be identified with the "reality" of God.

'Abdu'l-Bahá explains that:

"... there are two kinds of knowledge: the knowledge of the essence of a thing and the knowledge of its qualities."[2]

A man by nature cannot acquire knowledge about the essence of anything. Our knowledge is limited only to the attributes of things.

"The essence of a thing is known through its qualities; otherwise, it is unknown and hidden."[3]

For example, a table is known by its shape, colour, the type of the materials used in it, etc. Further information can be gleaned through the use of computer imaging, chemical analysis and electron microscopy. Otherwise, it is impossible to acquire any knowledge about the reality or the essence of the table.

An incomparably greater limitation applies to our knowledge of God. It is impossible for us to learn about the Reality of God. 'Abdu'l-Bahá emphasizes that *"... as things can only be known by their qualities and not by their essence, it is certain that the Divine Reality is unknown with regard to its essence and is known with regard to its attributes."*[4]

However, a direct knowledge of the attributes of God is also impossible for human beings due to major differences that exist between the nature and reality of the human and the Reality of God.

'Abdu'l-Bahá explains such differences as:

a) God is the "Pre-existent Reality" whereas man is the "phenomenal reality". This implies that God is ancient and eternal in contrast to the way that God has created man.

---

[1] 'Abdu'l-Bahá, Bahá'í World Faith, p. 323; *Some Answered Questions*, p. 222.
[2] 'Abdu'l-Bahá, *Some Answered Questions*, p. 220.
[3] 'Abdu'l-Bahá, *Some Answered Questions*, p. 220.
[4] 'Abdu'l-Bahá, *Some Answered Questions*, pp. 220–221.

b) God is infinite whereas man is finite. The finite cannot perceive the infinite. An example is the relationship between a drop of water and the ocean. A drop of water—even if it possessed the power of perception—could never understand the complexity and the nature of the ocean. *"No matter how far the human intelligence may advance, it is still but a drop, while divine omniscience is the ocean."*[1]

c) There is a difference of condition and degree of existence between man and God. For example, plants and animals are at different degrees of existence in the physical world. *"The plants, the trees, whatever progress they may make, cannot conceive of the power of sight or the powers of the other senses; and the animal cannot imagine the condition of man—that is to say, his spiritual powers."*[2]

---

[1] 'Abdu'l-Bahá, *The Promulgation of Universal Peace*, p. 66.
[2] 'Abdu'l-Bahá, *Some Answered Questions*, p. 221.

20.6 Activities

20.6.1 Double choice questions

For each statement given below, determine whether it is true or false.

		False	True
a)	The universe is static and no change occurs in it.	☐	☐
b)	A basic principle of physics is that a system changes when it is driven by a force.	☐	☐
c)	The universe has emerged from the nature as a result of chance and random incidents.	☐	☐
d)	The order and beauty observed in the universe could not have occurred by chance and accident.	☐	☐
e)	A Creator exists who has designed the universe and brought it into existence.	☐	☐
f)	It is logical to assume that a mighty force is driving evolution in the universe.	☐	☐
g)	The force driving the evolution of the universe is generated by nature.	☐	☐
h)	The force that has designed the universe and is driving it to perfection emanates from a Creator.	☐	☐
i)	In some situations, nature can act contrary to the universal laws.	☐	☐
j)	Belief in God has always been an intrinsic characteristic of man.	☐	☐
k)	Pre-historic humans did not believe in a Creator.	☐	☐
l)	Early religions taught that there was a god for every phenomenon in nature.	☐	☐
m)	There is only one God, though referred to by different names.	☐	☐
n)	We can have direct access to God if we persevere.	☐	☐

o) Our connection with God is through the Manifestations of God. ☐ ☐
p) We can understand the Reality of God. ☐ ☐
q) The universe evolves according to the Will of God. ☐ ☐
r) Man can acquire knowledge about the reality and attributes of things. ☐ ☐
s) God is infinite whereas man is finite. ☐ ☐

20.6.2 Short answer questions

1. Give an analogy to show that a system will change only when a force is applied to it.

_____
_____
_____
_____

2. Consider the force that is driving evolution in the universe. Answer the following questions:

   a) Is it possible to assume that nature is the source of the force? Explain?

   _____
   _____
   _____
   _____

   b) Is it possible to assume that man is generating this force? Explain.

   _____
   _____
   _____
   _____

c) What is the most logical way to explain the force that is driving evolution?

_____
_____
_____
_____

3. Explain why early humans believed in many gods.

_____
_____
_____
_____

4. What is the meaning of the oneness of God?

_____
_____
_____
_____

5. Give some examples of monotheistic religions.

_____
_____
_____
_____

6. How does God inform humanity of His Will and provide him with guidance?

_____
_____
_____
_____

7. Explain your understanding of the statement that "God is aware of His creation, has a Mind, a Will, and a Purpose".

8. What is the reality of an entity?

9. What is the attribute of an entity?

10. Are we able to acquire knowledge about the reality of things?

11. Explain why we cannot directly acquire knowledge of the attributes of God.

20.6.3 Project

Prepare a 10 minute talk to logically prove the existence of God. In addition to the materials provided in this chapter, you can use any other resources available in a library or on the Internet.

21 SPIRITUALITY

21.1 Introduction

Spirituality is the focus of this chapter. There are many definitions and interpretations of spirituality. A common thread among them all is the focus on spiritual ideals and qualities. Through spirituality, the thoughts, attitudes and deeds of an individual are influenced by the spiritual qualities of the soul. The life of the individual is also motivated and guided by the spiritual purpose of life. In this chapter we examine the effectiveness of science and religion in assisting us to develop spirituality through knowledge, volition and action.

In this chapter, you need to reflect on and understand the following key points:

a) The focus of spirituality is on developing spiritual qualities and ideals.
b) Attraction to spirituality has always been an integral part of human life.
c) Science is the systematic investigation, study and compilation of data about the physical world, thence formulating laws and theories about nature and the universe.
d) Scientific endeavours have a materialistic scope and cannot provide us with any understanding about human spiritual reality, the soul and the essence of the qualities embedded in it.
e) The formal education pursued in schools and universities is based on science and hence it often does not offer opportunities to nourish and develop our spiritual reality.

f) Religions have offered humanity the richest environment to experience spirituality and achieve spiritual development.

g) The primary aim of religion is to assist people to develop their inner capacities and their spiritual potential, while safeguarding the interests and promoting the unity of humanity.

21.2 Meaning of spirituality

In previous chapters we have studied and learned that the primary purpose of the physical life is to develop our hidden gifts and capacities towards achieving spiritual development and growth. Spiritual growth assists each of us to rise above the forces and conditions of our daily material existence. This attention to our spiritual reality and its progress is known as spirituality.

There are many definitions and interpretations of spirituality by different groups and in various contexts. You can familiarise yourself with these definitions through personal research and reflection. In this section, we focus on two processes that have been recognised as dominating spirituality:

a) The thoughts, attitudes and deeds of the individual are influenced by the spiritual qualities of the soul. Through this influence, the individual goes through a journey that begins with the transformation of his inner and private life and continues with the unfoldment of this change in his outer life i.e. what the individual says or does. For example, in the process of spiritual development, we can develop a more loving attitude towards people around us and show this love through our sincere, kind words and actions.

b) Our life is motivated and guided by the spiritual purpose of life. This also results in some fundamental changes to how we live and what we do. For example, we establish a better balance between the gratification of our physical needs and helping our friends to develop and grow. Work becomes more than earning money to pay for life's material expenses. Work offers a path of service and contribution to human civilization, while we also receive a physical reward to live a comfortable life.

From the above explanation, we can suggest that spirituality requires a coherent development of our inner capacities in all of our three realities towards realizing our spiritual potential.

Attraction to spiritually has always been an integral part of human life. Despite its non-tangible nature, people are usually aware of the impulse of spirituality within them. Over the course of human history, many thinkers and philosophers have shared their understanding of spirituality and of their experiences while following a spiritual journey.

In the context of knowledge, volition and action, attaining spirituality requires acquiring knowledge about it, developing a desire and motivation to attain it, and taking the necessary actions to achieve it by nurturing our spiritual reality, educating and cultivating our spiritual capacities; and applying the developed capacities in our attitudes, words and deeds.

In the remainder of this chapter, we explore the capacity of science and religion to assist us to develop spirituality.

21.3 Spirituality and science

Science is the systematic investigation, study and compilation of data about the physical world, thence formulating laws and theories about nature and the universe, using a scientific method of observation, experimentation, measurement and repeated testing to ensure the consistency of the results.

This definition implies that science and the scientific method have a materialistic scope. Hence, they cannot provide us with any understanding about human spiritual reality, the soul and the essence of the qualities embedded in it. The formal education pursued in schools and universities is based on science and hence it offers limited opportunities to nourish and develop our spiritual reality.

Physical education receives some regular attention at most schools. However, when it comes to the spiritual development of the student, religion is only offered in state primary schools as an optional subject taught by volunteers from various religious organisations. Any other regular, moral education in the school curriculum is taught as "ethics" and presented from a humanistic rather than a spiritual perspective. Only church-run schools have religious education as a regular part of the curriculum and, even then, it is rarely treated as a priority. Hence, the cultivation of the spiritual capacities is mostly ignored in formal education. The primary responsibility of schools and universities is to develop the intellectual capacities of students and give them the skills suitable for the job market.

This materialistic approach to education in present day society does not actively affirm the spiritual reality of man and the importance of its development. Intellectual development and material progress are critical for the advancement of civilization. However, when they occur in isolation from spiritual development, the well-being and happiness of an individual and of society are undermined. Intellectual development and material progress should assist humanity to reach its true spiritual purpose in life rather than becoming life's sole goal.

Hence, it can be concluded that neither science nor formal education have the necessary requirements to assist us in our spiritual development.

21.4 Spirituality and religion

Religions have offered humanity the richest environment within which to experience spirituality and to achieve spiritual development. Religion is as old as humanity. It is difficult to identify a time in human history when religion did not exist.

As previously discussed, the primary aim of religion is to assist people to develop their inner capacities, in particular their spiritual potentials. This is achieved by

- **Knowledge**: The teachings of religion provide a comprehensive insight into the spiritual reality of man and the dynamics of spirituality.
- **Volition**: The teachings of religion inspire and encourage an individual to endeavour on the path of spirituality. It provides a compelling motivation for spiritual development and a strong will to sustain the process.
- **Action**: The individual is empowered to develop spiritually through the revealed Writings and prayers of the religion. This is achieved through:
  - **Nourishment:** Religious sacred Writings and prayers provide nourishment for the development of the soul and of its inner capacities.
  - **Education**: While the primary focus of religious teachings is to cultivate spiritual capacities of the individual, strong directions and guidelines are also provided to ensure that the

intellectual and physical developments are aligned with and are supportive of spiritual development.
- **Application:** Religious faith empowers the individuals to apply the spiritual capacities acquired to both their inner and outer lives. The inner life includes thoughts and attitudes that represent the reality of the individual. The outer life is the manifestation of the aspired thoughts and attitudes in words and deeds, and our relationships with others.

21.5 Activities

21.5.1 Double choice questions

For each statement given below, determine whether it is true or false.

		False	True
a)	Spiritual growth assists an individual to work effectively.	☐	☐
b)	Spiritual growth assists an individual to rise above the daily material existence.	☐	☐
c)	Through spirituality, the thoughts, attitudes and deeds of an individual are influenced by the spiritual qualities of the soul.	☐	☐
d)	Spirituality results in more self-love and self-appreciation.	☐	☐
e)	Spirituality results in a better balance between the gratification of our physical needs and helping our friends to develop and grow.	☐	☐
f)	Spirituality requires a coherent development of the inner capacities in our spiritual and intellectual realities.	☐	☐
g)	Science is the systematic investigation, study and compilation of data about the physical world, thence formulating laws and theories that will cultivate our inner capacities.	☐	☐
h)	The scientific method consists of observation, experimentation, measurement, imagination and visualization.	☐	☐
i)	Formal school education provides us with sufficient opportunities to nourish and develop our spiritual reality.	☐	☐
j)	The materialistic approach to education in our society does not actively affirm the spiritual reality of man and the importance of its development.	☐	☐
k)	Religions have offered humanity the richest	☐	☐

environment in which to experience spirituality and to achieve spiritual development.

l) The main purpose of religion is to educate the intellectual reality of man. ☐ ☐

m) The main purpose of religion is to educate the spiritual reality of man. ☐ ☐

n) The main purpose of religion is to educate the physical reality of man. ☐ ☐

o) Religions provide a set of teachings and spiritual principles to nurture and empower individuals to realize their purpose in life. ☐ ☐

p) Religious sacred Writings and prayers provide nourishment for the development of the mind. ☐ ☐

q) Religious faith empowers individuals to apply their acquired spiritual capacities to both their inner and outer lives. ☐ ☐

21.5.2 Short answer questions

1. What is the meaning of spirituality?

_____
_____
_____
_____

2. How is the life of an individual affected by spirituality?

_____
_____
_____
_____

3. What is the meaning of science?

_____
_____

4. What is scientific method?

5. Can science assist us in nurturing our spiritual qualities?

6. How can religion assist individuals to acquire knowledge about spirituality?

7. How can religion assist individuals to develop volition for spirituality?

8. How can religion nurture the spiritual reality of an individual?

9. How can religion educate the spiritual reality of an individual?

10. How can religion motivate an individual to apply the cultivated spiritual qualities in their inner and outer lives?

11. Consider the two processes that determine spirituality:
    - The thoughts, attitudes and deeds of an individual are influenced by the spiritual qualities of the soul. Through this influence, the individual goes through a journey that begins with the transformation of his inner and private life and continues with the unfoldment of this change in his outer life i.e. what the individual says or does.
    - The life of an individual is motivated and guided by the spiritual purpose of life. This also results in some fundamental changes to how he lives and what he does.

    Read the following stories. In light of the above conditions, determine to what extent the life of the individual mentioned in each story is affected by spirituality. Explain the reasons.
    a) Annette's ambition in life is to be a nurse. She loves to help people. This will enable her to help those who really need help.

b) John believes that life is about having a good time and enjoying the best of everything that life offers. He would work hard to earn sufficient money to afford such a life style.

_____
_____
_____
_____

c) Adam's ambition in life is to be a teacher. He likes the job and also it provides him with the opportunity to educate the next generation. He believes this will be a great contribution to his society.

_____
_____
_____
_____

d) Jasmine is determined to realize her full potential and to excel in everything. Her struggle is not a competition against others but against her own self.

_____
_____
_____
_____

21.5.3 Project

Consider the two processes that determine spirituality. Reflect on the degree of your spirituality by comparing your inner and outer lives with the conditions mentioned above and respond to the following questions and comments:

a) What are your strong spiritual qualities?
b) Are your thoughts, attitudes and deeds affected by these qualities? Give some examples.

c) To what extent is your life influenced by the spiritual purpose of life defined in the previous chapters? Explain why.
d) Develop a plan to enhance your spirituality. You can use the knowledge, volition and action model in developing this plan.

22 Mystical Spirituality

22.1 Introduction

There are more advanced and mystical aspects of spirituality that unfold when another hidden gift of the soul, the spirit of faith, is cultivated. Religion and faith play a critical role in unfolding this gift. The spirit of faith is like a seed residing in the soul of every human being. The seed starts to grow when we recognize the station of a Manifestation of God and declare our belief in Him. The dynamics of mystical spirituality based on knowledge, volition and action strategy will be explored in this chapter.

In this chapter, you need to reflect on and understand the following key points:

a) The spirit of faith is like a seed residing in the soul of every human being.
b) The spirit of faith starts to grow when one recognizes the station of the Manifestation of God.
c) After the germination of the seed of the spirit of faith it should be nurtured through the Sacred Writings and prayers.
d) After physical death, the body returns to its origin, the earth, and the soul returns to its source, which is the spiritual world of God.
e) We recognise a Manifestation of God when we learn about His qualities and attributes.
f) The knowledge of God is a spiritual phenomenon that becomes imbedded in the receptive heart.
g) The knowledge of the attributes and beauty of God creates an attraction between the individual and God, known as the love of God.

h) The love of God motivates us yet another action—that of service to Him and to humanity.
i) The cycle of spiritual growth continues indefinitely as long as the individual consciously strives for spiritual growth.

22.2 Journey of the soul

In chapter 21 spirituality was defined as a process through which the thoughts, attitudes and deeds of the individual are influenced by the spiritual qualities of the soul. Virtues were mentioned as some of the hidden gifts of the soul, the cultivation of which contributes towards spiritual growth.

However, there are more advanced and mystical aspects of spirituality that unfold when another hidden gift of the soul, the spirit of faith, is cultivated. Religion and faith play a critical role in unfolding this gift.

The spirit of faith is like a seed planted in the soul of every human being. The seed of the spirit of faith starts to germinate as soon as one recognises the station of the Manifestation of God and declares one's belief in Him. From the outset, the nascent spirit of faith should be nurtured like a tender seedling. The Sacred Writings and the prayers revealed by the Manifestations of God are the nurturing food for the spirit of faith. Reading the Sacred Writings and prayers assists the growth of the spirit of faith to reach the point of certitude. At this stage, no trace of doubt regarding the station of the Manifestation of God will be left in the heart of the believer.

The spirit of faith has the power to transform the human soul. According to 'Abdu'l-Bahá, the soul becomes heavenly when it is embraced by the spirit of faith. He states that the human soul *"... unless assisted by the spirit of faith, does not become acquainted with the divine secrets and the heavenly realities. It is like a mirror which, although clear, polished and brilliant, is still in need of light. Until a ray of the sun reflects upon it, it cannot discover the heavenly secrets."*[1]

The soul is closely associated with the body while the individual is physically alive. When physical death occurs, the body returns to its origin, the earth. The soul also returns to its origin, which is the

---

[1] 'Abdu'l-Bahá, *Some Answered Questions*, pp. 208–209.

spiritual world of God. The journey of the soul from its birth to its return to God can be likened to the journey of an embryo that begins life in the womb as one cell, and develops into a fully formed foetus to be born into the physical world as a complete human being with the necessary organs and capacities for earthly life.

In a parallel process, the human soul begins its association with the human embryo at the time of conception, endowed with many capacities and gifts that must be cultivated and developed outside the womb, throughout childhood, adolescence and adulthood until the end of earthly life. Of all the capacities to be fostered during one's physical life, the utmost care should be given to one's spiritual development. The soul that has achieved the heights of its spiritual progress is then born into the world of God in a state of might and glory, with all the necessary qualities and attributes for its new stage of existence.

The condition of a child born in the physical world depends on the completion of its development in the womb. Similarly, the condition of the soul after death of the physical body depends on the degree of spiritual development it has achieved during its association with the body.

The journey of the soul is illustrated in Figure 22.1. All the possible developments destined for the growth of the soul are illustrated in this diagram. An individual has been given the free will to either undertake these stages or completely ignore them.

22.3 Dynamic of mystical spirituality

Spiritual development after recognition of the Manifestation of God is a journey driven by many mystical forces and spiritual processes. We call this stage of the development of the soul mystical spirituality.

Great attention is paid to the spirituality of the individual in the Bahá'í Faith, and Bahá'u'lláh has provided guidance and practical tools to help the individual soul on its spiritual journey.

Despite their spiritual nature, the processes of knowledge, volition and action play a critical role in developing mystical spirituality. In the following sections, the nature of knowledge, volition and action in advancing mystical spirituality will be explored.

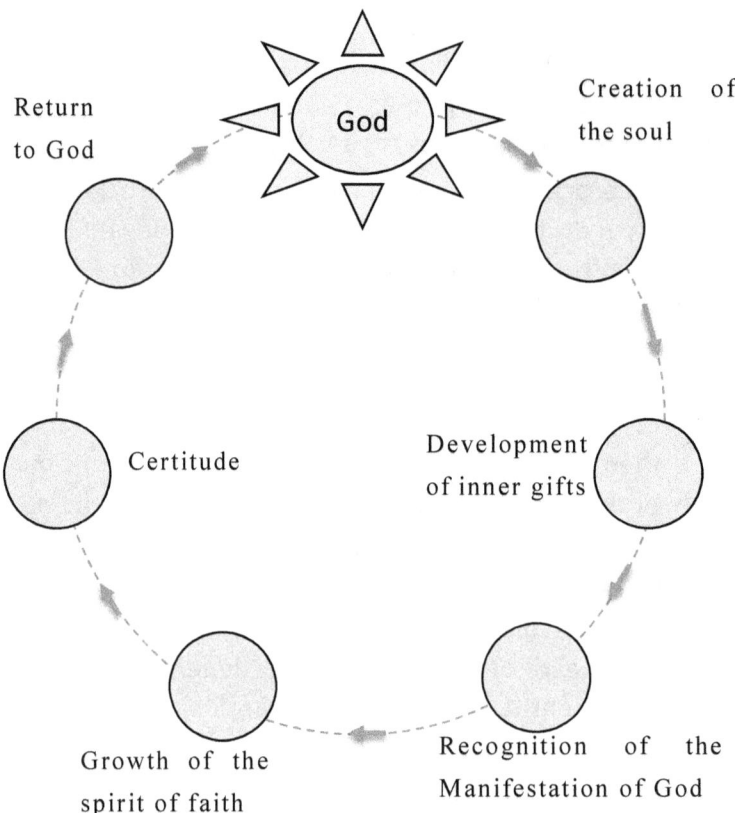

Figure 22.1 – Potential journey of the human soul

22.3.1 Knowledge: Knowledge of God

We cannot recognize the station of the Manifestation of God without knowledge about Him and the way He reflects the qualities and attributes of God. As we discussed in section 20.5, the Manifestations of God are like perfect mirrors, fully reflecting the attributes of God. Hence, for us to have knowledge of the Manifestations of God is the same as having knowledge of God.

Acquisition of knowledge is usually an intellectual process that occurs in the mind. The knowledge of God, however, is a spiritual phenomenon and is received and planted in the heart.

In chapter 9, we studied the association of the human soul with the physical body. This association occurs through various channels. We have mentioned that the mind is the result of the interaction between the mental powers of the soul, the human spirit and the brain. This is one channel of association between the soul and the human body. The soul also regulates the involuntary operations of the body organs and harmonises their functions through the human brain. This is another channel of association. Finally, the spiritual insight, intuition and inspiration of the soul are manifested in the human heart.

Hence, the human heart has spiritual perception and the power to discover but this is radically different from either sensory perception or discoveries made through the interaction of the mind and the power of reasoning. The factors limiting or strengthening this spiritual perception are also different from how the power of the intellect is enhanced. For example, the heart needs to be purified of the dross of the physical world that can obscure the spiritual discoveries of the heart. Such impurities include attachment to the material world, vices such as envy and cruelty; and misconceptions, superstitions and prejudices.

When the heart is not purified, it is difficult for an individual to either appreciate the attributes of God reflected in His Manifestation or recognise His station.

22.3.2 Volition: Love of God

The knowledge of the attributes and beauty of God creates an attraction between the individual and God through His Manifestation. This is known as the love of God and represents the desire to achieve nearness to God. According to 'Abdu'l-Bahá, the love of God is *"the fruit of human existence"* and its light *"shines in the lamp of the hearts of those who know God."*[1] It is the power that creates unity and harmony in life.

In *The Hidden Words*, Bahá'u'lláh describes the nature of God's love for us and how it gives rise to our love for Him. Some of those statements are described below:

- The love of God is within us—we must become aware of it:

    "My love is in thee, know it, that thou mayest find Me near unto thee."[2]

- The love of God for us is the cause of our creation:

---

[1] 'Abdu'l-Bahá, *Some Answered Questions*, pp. 300–301.
[2] Bahá'u'lláh, *The Hidden Words*, Arabic No. 10.

> *"I loved thy creation, hence I created thee. Wherefore, do thou love Me, that I may name thy name and fill thy soul with the spirit of life."*[1]

- Loving God is the key to receiving His love for us:

    > *"Love Me, that I may love thee. If thou lovest Me not, My love can in no wise reach thee."*[2]

- God's love is our Paradise:

    > *"Thy Paradise is My love; thy heavenly home, reunion with Me. Enter therein and tarry not."*[3]

- God's love is His stronghold for us:

    > *"My love is My stronghold; he that entereth therein is safe and secure, and he that turneth away shall surely stray and perish."*[4]

22.3.3 Action: Obedience and service

Our love of God results in a desire to carry out the laws prescribed by God. In *The Hidden Words*, Bahá'u'lláh clearly states that an obvious result of our love of Him is obedience to His commandments:

> *"O son of man!*
>
> *"Neglect not My commandments if thou lovest My beauty, and forget not My counsels if thou wouldst attain My good pleasure."*[5]

God's commandments provide a natural and essential framework for the behaviour of an individual. They are also the means to achieve inner peace and tranquillity. Bahá'u'lláh describes the laws of God as:

- *"The breath of life unto all created things."*[6]

- The *"lamps"* of God's loving providence and the *"keys"* of His mercy.

- *"The highest means for the maintenance of order in the world and the security of its peoples."*[7]

---

[1] Bahá'u'lláh, *The Hidden Words*, Arabic No. 4.
[2] Bahá'u'lláh, *The Hidden Words*, Arabic No. 5.
[3] Bahá'u'lláh, *The Hidden Words*, Arabic No. 6.
[4] Bahá'u'lláh, *The Hidden Words*, Arabic No. 9.
[5] Bahá'u'lláh: *The Hidden Words*, Arabic No. 39.
[6] Bahá'u'lláh, *Gleanings from the Writings of Bahá'u'lláh*, p. 331.
[7] Bahá'u'lláh, *The Kitáb-i-Aqdas*, pp. 19–20.

Our love of God also sparks another response in us, namely the desire to arise in service to Him. This is the action of carrying out voluntary work to advance the Cause of God, and thus benefit humanity. In the same way as obedience to the laws of God, service to His Cause and to humanity plays a critical role in the spiritual development of an individual. Service is described as a plough, which ploughs the physical soil when the seeds are sown.[1] This enriches the soil and results in a stronger growth of the seed.

Similarly, service ploughs up the soil of the heart and leads to a stronger growth of the spirit of faith, a deeper knowledge of God, and a stronger love of God. This in turn creates a stronger desire in the individual to obey the laws of God and serve Him more fervently. Hence, the cycle of spiritual growth continues indefinitely as long as the individual consciously strives for spiritual growth. This is illustrated in Figure 22.2.

The process mentioned above represents just one approach to mystical spirituality as guided by the Sacred Writings of the major religions, particularly the Bahá'í Faith. People around the world pursue spirituality through other avenues and means. You can learn about these methods through your personal research.

---

[1] Shoghi Effendi, cited in *The Compilation of Compilations*, Vol. II (*Living the Life*), No. 1334, pp. 24–25.

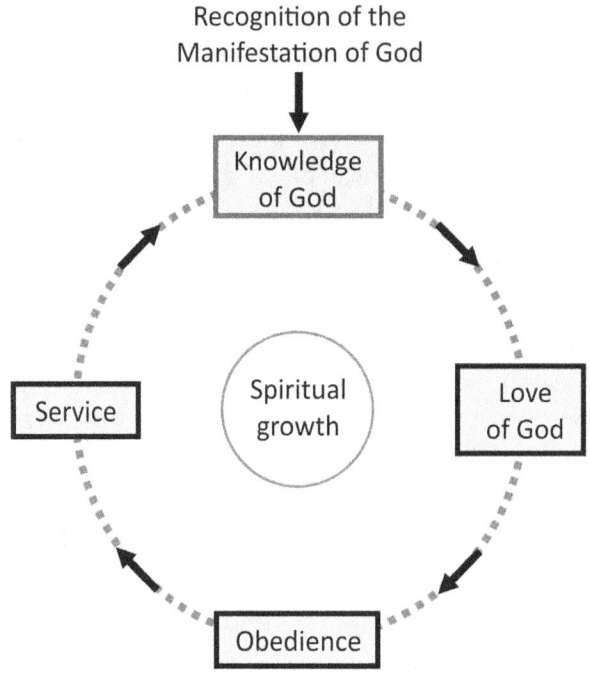

22.2 – The process of mystical spirituality

22.4 Activities

22.4.1 Multiple Choice Questions

1. When does the mystical spirituality start?_____.
    A. At conception
    B. At birth
    C. When we accept the Manifestation of God for the age
    D. None of the above

2. What role does the individual have in his spiritual growth?_____.
    A. To exert sustained efforts to develop divine attitudes, qualities and behaviour
    B. Acceptance of the Manifestation of God
    C. To say prayers
    D. All of the above

3. How do we know God?_____.
    A. Through meditation and prayer
    B. By recognizing His Manifestation
    C. Through suffering and self-sacrifice
    D. None of the above

4. How can one acquire spiritual capacities? _____.
    A. Spiritual capacities are gifts from God
    B. Spiritual capacities are obtained through education
    C. Spiritual capacities are achieved through prayer and meditation
    D. All of the above

5. How does spiritual growth occur?_____.
    A. Through the knowledge of God
    B. Through the love of God
    C. Through obedience to the laws of the Manifestation of God
    D. All of the above

6. How does service help spiritual growth?_____.
    A. It is a catalyst that facilitates spiritual development.
    B. It ploughs up the soil of the heart.
    C. It puts the spiritual qualities into practice and tests the degree to which these have been developed.
    D. All of the above

7. How long does the process of spiritual growth continue?_____.

A. It continues as long as the individual consciously strives for spiritual growth
B. It ends when one has recognized the Manifestation of God
C. It ends when one starts to serve
D. It ends when one has developed detachment from material things

8. God's love for us _____.
   A. is within us and we must become aware of it
   B. enables us to reach paradise
   C. enables us to receive God's love
   D. All of the above

9. Without God's love _____.
   A. material civilization would be destroyed
   B. spiritual union would be lost
   C. science and technology would not develop
   D. All of the above

10. The laws of God are _____.
    A. The breath of life to all creatures
    B. The lamp of God's-loving providence and the keys of His mercy
    C. The highest means for maintaining order and security
    D. All of the above

11. What is man's knowledge of God?_____.
    A. Our knowledge of the attributes of God
    B. Our knowledge of the essence of God
    C. Our knowledge of the Holy Spirit
    D. All of the above

12. How do we learn about the attributes of God?_____.
    A. Through meditation and prayer
    B. By studying books written about God
    C. By learning about the attributes of the Manifestation of God
    D. All of the above

13. Why did God create man?_____.
    A. Because of His love for him
    B. Because He needed a creation
    C. Because it was God's plan

D. All of the above

22.4.2 Short answer questions

1. What is mystical spirituality?

2. What is the spirit of faith?

3. When does the spirit of faith start to grow?

4. What is the effect of the spirit of faith on the soul?

5. Describe the journey of the soul from its birth to the death of the physical body.

6. Why is the acquisition of the knowledge of God a mystical phenomenon?

___

7. What can prevent the heart from receiving the knowledge of God?

___

8. What is the love of God?

___

9. Describe your understanding of the following *Hidden Words* of Bahá'u'lláh on God's love for us.

   a) *"My love is in thee, know it, that thou mayest find Me near unto thee."*[1]

   ___

   b) *"I loved thy creation, hence I created thee. Wherefore, do thou love Me, that I may name thy name and fill thy soul with the spirit of life."*[2]

---

[1] Bahá'u'lláh, *The Hidden Words*, Arabic No. 10.
[2] Bahá'u'lláh, *The Hidden Words*, Arabic No. 4.

_____
_____
_____
_____

    c) *"Love Me, that I may love thee. If thou lovest Me not, My love can in no wise reach thee."*[1]

_____
_____
_____
_____

    d) *"Thy Paradise is My love; thy heavenly home, reunion with Me. Enter therein and tarry not."*[2]

_____
_____
_____
_____

    e) *"My love is My stronghold; he that entereth therein is safe and secure, and he that turneth away shall surely stray and perish."*[3]

_____
_____
_____

10. Why is obedience to the laws of God important for spiritual growth?

_____
_____

---

[1] Bahá'u'lláh, *The Hidden Words*, Arabic No. 5.
[2] Bahá'u'lláh, *The Hidden Words*, Arabic No. 6.
[3] Bahá'u'lláh, *The Hidden Words*, Arabic No. 9.

11. What is service?

12. How does service intensify spiritual growth?

13. Describe the cycle of mystical spirituality.

22.4.3 Project

Design a poster to illustrate the dynamics of mystical spirituality.

a) On the poster describe all the stages of the journey.
b) Have you had any personal experience of any of the stages of the mystical spirituality? Describe your personal experience.

23 TRUE HAPPINESS

23.1 Introduction

Happiness is probably the most celebrated human experience after love. Most of our endeavours, such as the pursuit of wealth, success, education and relationships, are aimed at achieving happiness. This chapter explores the meaning of happiness and identifies two main types of happiness: transient happiness and true happiness. In the following sections the characteristics of each type of happiness will be studied and differences between them will be highlighted.

In this chapter, you need to reflect on and understand the following key points:

a) Happiness can be defined as the state of well-being characterized by emotions ranging from contentment to intense joy. The two main types of happiness are transient happiness and true happiness.
b) Transient happiness is a feeling that we experience when our physical needs and desires are satisfied.
c) Transient happiness is limited and short-lived.
d) True happiness is a condition that is reached through spiritual progress.
e) True-happiness is unlimited and fathomless.
f) Transient and true happiness play complementary roles in the life of an individual so long as transient happiness is pursued with moderation.
g) Divine religions provide the foundations for true happiness.
h) Inner peace is achieved when we do not have any conflict within ourselves.

23.2 Happiness

Happiness is probably the most celebrated human experience after love. In our materialistic society, most of the effort exerted by the individual towards the pursuit of wealth, success, education and relationships are aimed at achieving happiness. However, happiness, like justice and love, has proved difficult to describe and it is open to interpretation. There are many questions asked about happiness:

- What exactly is happiness?
- How can it be achieved?
- What course of actions, which choices, and what life styles bring the highest happiness?
- Is happiness necessary for a good life?
- Does it matter how we achieve happiness?

Research reveals many definitions for happiness, which can be summarized as a state of well-being characterized by emotions ranging from contentment to intense joy. Here are some of those definitions:

- "[To be happy] is to really to enjoy the good things in life, if and when they come your way; to experience pleasure, enthusiasm, satisfaction ... to be truly joyful, 'high' when things go right for you."[1]
- "True happiness is a profound, enduring feeling of contentment, capability and centredness. It's a rich sense of well-being that comes from knowing that you can deal productively and creatively with all that life offers—both the good and the bad. It's being your internal self and responding to your real needs, rather than the demands of others. And it's a deep sense of engagement—living in the moment and enjoying life's bounty."[2]
- "To be happy is to be generally 'pleased with life'."[3]
- "Happiness ... involves realising one's important values, when these are justified relative to the best standard of justification."[4]

---

[1] D. Lykken, *Happiness*, p. 7, New York: St. Martin's Press, 1999.
[2] R. Foster and G. Hicks, *How We Choose to be Happy*, p. 3, New York: Penguin Putnam, Inc., 1999.
[3] D. G. Myers, *The Pursuit of Happiness*, pp. 23–24, New York: Avon Books, Inc., 1992.
[4] L. McFall, "Happiness, rationality, and individual ideals", *Review of Metaphysics*, 23 (March 1984): p. 596.

Each definition of happiness has an underlying philosophical principle that provides answers to the questions on happiness asked above. A theory of happiness consists of three elements:

a) **Definition of happiness**: It clarifies the meaning of happiness, and what it consists of.
b) **An approach to happiness**: It describes what activities, relationships and experiences result in happiness.
c) **Justification of the approach**: It explains why and how those activities, relationships and experiences make us happy.

Broadly, 'Abdu'l-Bahá identifies two types of happiness: physical and spiritual:

"Happiness consists of two kinds; physical and spiritual. The physical happiness is limited; its utmost duration is one day, one month, one year. It hath no result. Spiritual happiness is eternal and unfathomable."[1]

Physical and spiritual happiness are also referred to as transient and true happiness, respectively. In the following sections, the characteristics of transient and true happiness will be explored.

23.3 Transient happiness

Transient happiness is a feeling that we experience when our physical needs and desires are satisfied. The need can be biological and physical, or emotional. It is driven by our desire for power, wealth or anything else that we love to have.

A cold drink brings us a great deal of joy when we are walking outside on a hot day and are feeling thirsty. However, this joy diminishes as our thirst is quenched. Our favourite food will also give us a great deal of pleasure when we are hungry. At the same time, we can get sick of that food when we have eaten it in excess.

We often say that we would be happy if we had a new bike, or a new television or a new computer or some such other new possession. However, if our desire is fulfilled, the novelty of these possessions soon wears off and our happiness correspondingly diminishes. Becoming the school captain or winning a particular competition might be our dream. Accomplishing the dream will give

---

[1] 'Abdu'l-Bahá, *Bahá'í Scriptures*, p. 472.

us happiness for just a short period until we start to take our achievement for granted.

The above examples show that transient happiness is a temporary and short-lived experience, which ends when our biological needs and emotional selfish desires are fulfilled. It is quite natural to respond positively to our physical needs and to ensure that we maintain our health and well-being. We need to have healthy food and drink, and to abstain from what can temporarily or permanently harm our body. Rest and sleep are essential for us to maintain a strong immune system, and to work and study effectively.

The key to our wellbeing, however, is moderation in the pursuit of transient happiness only to the extent of satisfying our needs. Unfortunately, negative traits such as greed, self-indulgence, and the seeking of wealth and power for their own sake, can drive us to excessively pursue our self-centred, materialistic and egoistic desires. These negative traits can be extremely counter-productive and result in unhappiness, hardship and misery for us and for others.

Unfortunately, in today's materialistic society, the pursuit of transient happiness is strongly encouraged and promoted. We are praised for having the "best", the "fastest", the "biggest", the "most luxurious", etc. Television programmes, advertising and printed media constantly sell us the message to spend more and accumulate consumer goods, with the promise that they will bring us happiness. Hence, many people become trapped in a vicious cycle of seeking transient happiness that usually results in disappointment, disillusion and despair.

23.4 True happiness

True happiness is a condition that is achieved through spiritual progress. This requires an understanding of the origin and nature of our spiritual self, and the purpose of our existence, combined with genuine efforts towards fulfilling that purpose. To reach such an understanding we need to find convincing responses to questions such as:

- Who and what am I?
- Am I loved?
- Am I the result of an accident or is there a purpose for my existence?

- What is the purpose if there is one?
- How can I fulfil that purpose?
- How should I prepare for it?

'Abdu'l-Bahá explains that the supreme honour and real happiness of individual "... *lie in self-respect, in high resolves and noble purposes, in integrity and moral quality, in immaculacy of mind ...*" not "... *in the accumulation, by whatever means may offer, of worldly goods.*"[1] The conditions defined by 'Abdu'l-Bahá for true happiness are spiritual conditions that are achieved through spiritual growth.

Achieving true happiness requires an understanding of the self, pursuing a vision and purpose in life, and rising above the physical world and selfish desires. Hence, it is a quest for transcendence and a journey beyond our animal nature towards fulfilling our higher purpose as a human being. It requires self-respect and a noble purpose, integrity and moral qualities in our lives. The ultimate true happiness is a state of contentment with self, and tranquillity. True happiness is much more stable than transient happiness. These spiritual conditions are fulfilled when the mystical journey of an individual has advanced and spiritual growth occurs.

The limitations of transient happiness and its nature do not imply that it is unnecessary. Transient and true happiness play complementary roles in the life of an individual so long as transient happiness is pursued with moderation.

The Manifestations of God, as perfect Teachers, provide a complementary education for our physical, intellectual and spiritual selves. They provide a framework for a balanced and moderate attention to our physical self in order to attend to our physical needs. At the same time They provide teachings that are conducive to our true happiness and development.

According to 'Abdu'l-Bahá, the purpose of statements He makes on happiness, "*...is to make it abundantly clear that the Divine religions, the holy precepts, the heavenly teachings, are the unassailable basis of human happiness, and that the peoples of the world can hope for no real relief or deliverance without this one great remedy.*"[2]

---

[1] 'Abdu'l-Bahá, *The Secret of Divine Civilization*, p. 19.
[2] 'Abdu'l-Bahá, *The Secret of Divine Civilization*, p. 99.

He also points out: *"... human happiness consists only in drawing closer to the Threshold of Almighty God, and in securing the peace and well-being of every individual member, high and low alike, of the human race; and the supreme agencies for accomplishing these two objectives are the excellent qualities with which humanity has been endowed."* [1]

23.5 Inner peace

Inner peace or inner happiness is the ideal state for a human being. Inner peace is achieved when we do not have any conflict within ourselves. It is easier to maintain inner peace when we experience true happiness.

Inner conflict most commonly occurs when the influences of our different realities on our moral choices and pursuit of our desires are at variance.

In making choices or resolving a moral dilemma, the three aspects of the self contribute towards a solution through a balancing of moral knowledge, moral feeling and moral behaviour, as mentioned in the previous chapters. Inner conflict results when the moral knowledge, feeling and behaviour do not lead to the same solution. For example, when faced with a moral choice, we might know the ethically right decision, but we act against this knowledge because we have a different desire. This can result in an inner conflict. Here is a more detailed example of an inner conflict.

James finds a wallet at school. He opens the wallet and finds a significant amount of money in it. There is also an identification card in the wallet with the owner's name.

James needs to make one of these choices:
- Take the wallet and its contents to the school's office so that it can be returned to its owner.
- Take the money and destroy the wallet without mentioning it to anyone.

James knows that the morally right decision is to return the wallet, and he would love to be honest. However, he would like to use the money to buy an iPod.

---

[1] 'Abdu'l-Bahá, *The Secret of Divine Civilization*, p. 60.

If, despite his moral knowledge and moral feeling, James did not return the wallet, his action would contradict his knowledge and his feelings. This would result in inner conflict, and demolish his inner peace.

If, on the contrary, James decided to be honest and return the wallet, his knowledge, volition and action would be in harmony and he would avoid inner conflict.

23.6 Activities

23.6.1 Double choice questions

For each statement given below, determine whether it is true or false.

		False	True
a)	There are different definitions and interpretations for happiness.	☐	☐
b)	Transient happiness can be experienced when our physical needs are satisfied.	☐	☐
c)	True happiness can be experienced when our ego achieves its objectives.	☐	☐
d)	Transient happiness lasts forever.	☐	☐
e)	True happiness is infinite.	☐	☐
f)	True happiness is experienced when our intellectual and spiritual needs are satisfied.	☐	☐
g)	Transient happiness and true happiness are both necessary and complementary.	☐	☐
h)	Indulgence in the pursuit of transient happiness is acceptable.	☐	☐
i)	Inner peace can be achieved when our physical, intellectual and spiritual selves are in perfect harmony.	☐	☐
j)	Virtues assist in achieving inner peace.	☐	☐
k)	We should never pursue transient happiness.	☐	☐
l)	Spirituality leads to true happiness.	☐	☐
m)	Human happiness is achieved by accumulating wealth.	☐	☐
n)	Divine religions provide the foundations for true happiness.	☐	☐

23.6.2 Short answer questions

1. What is a general definition of happiness?

_____

_____

2. What is the theory of happiness?

3. Describe the meaning of the following elements of the theory of happiness:
    a) Definition of happiness:

    b) An approach to happiness:

    c) Justification of the approach:

4. What is transient happiness?

5. What is true happiness?

6. How can we achieve true happiness?

7. What is inner peace?

   _____
   _____
   _____

8. How can we achieve inner peace?

   _____
   _____
   _____
   _____

23.6.3 Projects

1. Compile a list of 5 things that make you happy and determine whether each resulting happiness is transient or true.
2. Describe an incident in your life that brought you inner conflict. Identify the positions that your intellectual-self, spiritual-self and physical-self assumed in the incident. How did you resolve the inner conflict?

24 Building an Ever Advancing Civilization

24.1 Introduction

Bahá'u'lláh states that humanity was created to carry forward an ever advancing civilization.[1] The purpose of our physical life is to cultivate the innate gifts in our physical, intellectual and spiritual realities; and to contribute the acquired qualities, virtues and skills towards advancing human civilization. In this last chapter of the book we will explore how you can contribute towards the process of building civilization. In contrast to the development of advanced educational methods to release human physical and intellectual capacities, our society has no systematic process in place to cultivate the human spiritual capacities and to stimulate spiritual growth. The formal education system completely overlooks the spiritual nature of the human being. Despite this, you can contribute to the process of building civilization by committing yourself to the spiritual education and empowerment of children and junior youth.

In this chapter, you need to reflect on and understand the following key points:

a) Humanity has collectively manifested characteristics that are not found in any other species on the earth.
b) Human civilization and culture are the product of the inquiring nature of the human mind.
c) Human history clearly demonstrates that major religions have been the driving force behind the emergence of great human civilizations and cultures.

---

[1] Bahá'u'lláh, *Gleanings from the Writings of Bahá'u'lláh*, p. 215.

d) There are few opportunities in our generally materialistic society to release our spiritual capacities and advance our spiritual growth.
e) You can play a major role in the spiritual education of humanity as your contribution towards building an ever advancing civilization.
f) You can contribute to this spiritual enterprise by committing to the spiritual education and empowerment of children and junior youth.

24.2 Human civilization

As mentioned in the previous chapters, one of the purposes of human physical life is to cultivate the innate gifts in our physical, intellectual and spiritual realities; and to acquire the virtues, skills and qualities that will enable us to contribute towards building an ever-advancing civilization.

As a result of such contributions, humanity has collectively manifested unique characteristics not found in any other species on the earth. An example is human culture and civilization. In the past the outward life of man differed little from that of animals, but inwardly he had the potential for discovery and innovation. Archaeological findings indicate that the dawn of human physical discoveries was the development of stone tools about two million years ago. This was followed by the discovery and control of fire about five hundred thousand years ago.

Human civilization and culture are the product of the inquiring nature of the human mind over the two million years of its development and evolution. The process of discovery, though sustained and accelerating, has been irregular and non-linear. Every new understanding, concept, invention and discovery has been a cornerstone and foundation for further discoveries and innovations.

The nature of the collective intellectual and spiritual evolution of man is similar to the development of a human infant. The earliest stages of a baby's growth follows the parallel process found in the young of the animal kingdom, which not only become familiar with their surroundings through their often much more acute senses but also quickly gain the use of their limbs and generally grow more rapidly. However the physical development of human infants, though slower, involves an incomparably higher level of mental capacity that soon outstrips the abilities of even the most intelligent of mature adult animals. It is well understood now that discovery is an intrinsic characteristic of a human being from the time of his birth. In the first four months of life, an infant learns to take an interest in its environment through the senses of sight, hearing, touch and smell. This attitude of enquiry evolves and intensifies as the individual matures into a more complex process of systematic discovery of the world through the acquisition, organization and representation of knowledge; as well as through innovation and the discovery of new concepts and theories.

In contrast to such fundamental changes in human life and the emergence of advanced civilizations and cultures that have learnt to harness the powers of nature, animals continue to follow their instincts and either become physically adapted to their environment by natural selection or succumb to extinction. Hence, contrary to atheistic theories that reject the spiritual nature of man and his distinction from the animal, human civilization and culture can be considered as one of the strong evidences of the victory of the human mind and soul over instinct and matter.

24.3 Human civilization and religion

Human history clearly demonstrates that the major religions have been the driving force behind the emergence of all great human civilizations and cultures. The nature of contribution of religion to philosophy, civilization and culture has evolved in parallel with human material, intellectual and spiritual development.

According to 'Abdu'l-Bahá: *"... the philosophers of Greece such as Pythagora. s, acquired the major part of their philosophy, both divine and material, from the disciples of Solomon. And Socrates after having eagerly journeyed to meet with some of Israel's most illustrious scholars and divines, on his return to Greece established the concept of the oneness of God and the continuing life of the human soul after it has put off its elemental dust."*[1]

Zoroastrianism was the state religion of the Archaemenid, Parthian, and Sasanian empires, and was adopted by the Persian kings as their religion. The Persian Empire blossomed as a result of the teachings of Zoroastrianism, and it spread to include Babylon, Palestine and Egypt.

---

[1] 'Abdu'l-Bahá, *The Secret of Divine Civilization*, p. 77.

The laws revealed by Moses have become the basis of common law in many countries. Christianity was the dominant force in western culture before the advent of the modern science. Islám gave birth to the greatest culture that humanity had witnessed prior to the industrial revolution. Through the transforming influence of Islám, the *"... Arabs then excelled all the peoples of the world in science and the arts, in industry and invention, in philosophy, government and moral character."*[1]

The Manifestations of God have progressively revealed the purpose of God for humanity. Through true education They have released the capacities of individuals, given humanity a vision of a materially and spiritually prosperous society, and motivated man to work towards that vision. Each Revelation has thus advanced human civilization to a consecutively higher level.

24.4 Engaging in a spiritual enterprise

Discoveries and inventions over the last one hundred and fifty years have revolutionised the way we live compared to that of our ancestors. Our material civilization has significantly progressed through scientific and technological developments and led to the generation of great material wealth for the fortunate minority. We have also learned how to release the physical and intellectual capacities inherent in every individual through effective educational processes. Schools and universities in our modern societies train the human resources needed to maintain and further advance our material civilization.

However, with such emphasis placed on these great material advances, there are fewer opportunities in society for the release of our spiritual capacities and advancing our spiritual growth. Formal education mostly overlooks the spiritual aspects of an individual. Consequently, many people are not aware of their noble station, stay ignorant of their true nature, remain devoid of spiritual qualities, and develop poor relationships with others.

In our materialistic society, the pursuit of transient happiness is the main pre-occupation of many people. Corruption, injustice, jealousy

---

[1] 'Abdu'l-Bahá, *The Secret of Divine Civilization*, p. 88.

and envy are widespread. Despite great material affluence, many people live in misery and unhappiness.

It is critical that equal attention be given to the spiritual development of every individual in order to resolve the many complex challenges that humanity faces. For example, when our spiritual development as a society has caught up with our technological and scientific development, the wealth that has been generated will be shared more justly among the poorer countries who have not got the resources or whose resources have been plundered in the process of creating that wealth.

You can play a major role in the spiritual education of humanity as part of your contribution towards building an ever advancing civilization. This will be in addition to your material and intellectual contributions as you serve your society in your employment and profession. You can contribute to this spiritual enterprise by committing yourself to the spiritual education and empowerment of children and junior youth. We look at the nature of such contributions in the following sections.

24.4.1 Spiritual education of children

We give a great deal of attention to the physical well-being of children from the time of their birth. We ensure that they receive adequate nourishment and protect them against any harm. In most of countries, children are vaccinated against dangerous diseases and are regularly under the care of a physician.

The intellectual development of children also receives a great deal of attention from their early days. There is a wealth of books, games and computer software available for children to stimulate their intellectual growth. There are also advanced pedagogical methods developed to teach mathematics and reading to children much younger than the traditional starting school age.

That is all very commendable. However, we should also take similar or even greater care of the spiritual development of children. After all, in the same way as the physical body, the human soul, also needs nourishment and training in order to develop all its capacities. This should start from infancy. 'Abdu'l-Bahá warns us: *"Certainly, certainly, neglect not the education of the children. Rear them to be possessed of spiritual qualities, and be assured of the gifts and favours of the Lord."*[1]

Bahá'í communities around the world run training programmes for teachers of children's spiritual education classes as part of their community building process. These classes are open to children of all backgrounds and often run in collaboration with the parents. The lessons draw on the teachings of the Bahá'í Faith, and aim to instil in children the love of God and His Manifestations. The content of the class is based both on the sacred verses and conversation about the questions and issues that children face. Children are also encouraged to apply spiritual principles such as love, unity and justice to their own lives, their families and their friends.

You can approach the Bahá'ís where you live and express your interest in helping with their programmes. The training program is short and you will be supported as you become engaged in running the classes.

24.4.2 Spiritual education of junior youth

We refer to young people between the ages of 12–14 as junior youth. This is a special stage in the development of an individual between childhood and becoming a youth, and represents the early years of adolescence. It is during this period, when junior youth are going through significant physical, intellectual, emotional and social changes, that preparing them for a deeper cultivation of their spiritual capacities is most crucial.

The most pronounced changes include: increased independence from parents while developing greater dependence on peers; greater potential for moral reasoning; increased ability to distinguish right from wrong; and a greater concern for physical appearance.

Early adolescence is a time when significant changes occur in the brain leading to increased cognitive ability. Youngsters start to develop advanced reasoning and abstract thinking skills, and have a greater tendency to process their own thoughts.

An important development in the life of junior youth is the gradual process of forming their identities, where they learn what and who they are as individuals. During times of stability, young people fit into

---

[1] 'Abdu'l-Bahá, *The Compilation of Compilations*, vol. I, p. 374.

the patterns and behaviours established by previous generations. Currently, however, we are living in times of significant global social changes that result in new social issues, conditions and relationships. Uncertainty and transition are the hallmarks of our societies.

Hence, forming their individual identities has become a critical task for every junior youth. The traditional sources of collective social identity have lost their relevance and acceptance. The patterns of behaviour of older people are no longer reliable sources of guidance. Junior youth feel personal responsibility for their lives and bear the risks associated with a rapidly changing society. They have to make choices about their actions in an uncertain environment.

Spiritual empowerment of junior youth helps to provide them with the necessary frame of mind, qualities and attitudes to develop a sound identity and to effectively respond to the critical changes that are occurring in them.

Bahá'í communities around the world also run spiritual empowerment program for junior youth. The aim of this program is to assist junior youth in developing their identities by nurturing their spiritual and intellectual capacities in a coherent, genuine and loving way. The spiritual empowerment program is offered in small groups in a neighbourhood or a village often run by an older youth.

The junior youth program endeavours to instil in junior youth the sense of a twofold moral purpose:

i) To take charge of their own intellectual and spiritual growth
ii) To contribute to the transformation of society.

This program strives to achieve the following goals:

a) Assist the junior youth to enhance their powers of expression.
b) Reinforce a moral structure that will serve them throughout their lives and will help them in distinguishing wrong from right.
c) Cultivate the concept of service in the junior youth and encourage them to engage in different acts of community service.
d) Encourage the junior youth to explore and develop their talents and hidden abilities, in an effort to build their capacity for service to others.

You can engage in running junior youth groups by completing a short training program offered by the Bahá'í community where you live.

24.5 Activities

24.5.1 Double choice questions

For each statement given below, determine whether it is true or false.

		False	True
a)	Humanity has collectively manifested characteristics that are not found in any other species on earth.	☐	☐
b)	Human civilization and culture are the product of human instincts.	☐	☐
c)	Human civilization and culture can be considered as strong evidences of the superior human physical reality.	☐	☐
d)	Socrates established his philosophy after meeting some of Israel's most illustrious scholars and divines.	☐	☐
e)	The Persian Empire blossomed through the influence of the teachings of Moses.	☐	☐
f)	Islám gave birth to the greatest culture that humanity had witnessed before the industrial revolution.	☐	☐
g)	The Manifestations of God have progressively revealed the purpose of God for humanity.	☐	☐
h)	Formal education provides a comprehensive program for the spiritual education of children.	☐	☐
i)	We have learned well how to release the physical and intellectual capacities inherent in every individual through effective educational processes.	☐	☐
j)	The human soul, similarly to the physical body, needs nourishment and training in order to reveal all its capacities.	☐	☐

24.5.2 Short answer questions

1. What is meant by the term "human civilization"?

2. How has human civilization advanced?

3. What are the similarities between the collective intellectual and spiritual evolution of man and the development of a human infant?

4. How does human evolution compare to animal evolution?

5. What has been the role of religion in the development of human civilization? Give three examples.

6. How is spiritual education dealt with in formal education programmes?

7. What are the negative characteristics of our materialistic society?

8. Why is the spiritual education of children very important?

9. What are the main characteristics of junior youth? List them in bullet form.

10. How does spiritual education help junior youth?

_____
_____
_____
_____
_____

24.5.3 Project

Develop a plan on how you are going to contribute to human civilization both materially, intellectually and spiritually. Use the following questions to guide you in your plan:

a) What profession are you going to pursue in serving your community?
b) How are you going to develop the necessary capacities and skills for this profession?
c) How are going to contribute towards the spiritual development of people around you?
d) Which age group are you interested in helping?
e) How are you going to acquire the necessary knowledge and skills to run spiritual empowerment classes?
f) How are you going to start your classes?

APPENDIX-FURTHER RESOURCES

In this appendix, some resources for your further study are provided.

Inspiring examples

This is a list of inspiring biographies. The examples show how some people have contributed to building a better society. There are many other similar books that you can find by browsing through your school or town library, and the Internet. You can plan a schedule to read these books.

a) Helen Keller, *Story of my life*, Barnes and Noble.
b) Michael Elsohn Ross, *A world of her own: 24 Amazing Women Explorers and Adventurers*, Barnes and Noble.
c) Clara Ingram Judson, *Abraham Lincoln, Friend of the People*, Sterling Point Books Series.
d) Regine Stokke, Henriette Larsen (Translator), *Regine's Book: A Teen Girl's Last Words*.
e) Elizabeth Goldman, *Believers, Spiritual Leaders of the World*.

Guides on health and nutrition

The list below provides some examples of books which can help you to look after your physical self. There are many other similar books that you can find by browsing your school library, town library and the Internet.

a) Robert J. Sullivan, Deena Cloud, *The Human Body – How it works: Digestion and Nutrition*, Barnes & Noble.

b) *Healthy Eating – A Guide to Nutrition Series*: This is a series of six books by various authors and includes Lori A. Smolin's *Basic Nutrition* and Toney Allman's *Nutrition and Disease Prevention*, Barnes & Noble
c) Meghann Foye, *Seventeen 500 Health & Fitness Tips: Eat Right, Work out smart, and Look Great!*, Barnes & Noble.

Resources on spiritual journey

A list of resources that can provide you with a better insight into your spiritual journey is provided below. These material are available both electronically on the Internet or in print.

a) Bahá'u'lláh, *The Hidden Words:* This is a small book that represents the ethical core of the Revelation of Bahá'u'lláh and provides guidance for the spiritual growth of the individual.
b) Bahá'u'lláh, *The Seven Valleys*: This book describes various stages in the spiritual journey of an individual towards God.
c) 'Abdu'l-Bahá, *Some Answered Questions*: This book is the result of conversations between 'Abdu'l-Bahá and Laura Clifford Barney that occurred during 1904–1906. It provides a collection of answers on various issues related to the nature of the human and other spiritual matters.
d) 'Abdu'l-Bahá, *Paris Talks*: This is a collection of Talks given by 'Abdu'l-Bahá in Paris in 1911–1912 covering various spiritual concepts and teachings.
e) Henry A. Weil, *Drops from the Ocean*: This book provides an inner meaning of words, terms and phrases relating to human spiritual nature and growth derived from the Bahá'í Writings. It also shows how these concepts can be applied in everyday situations.
f) Henry A. Weil, *Closer than your Life-vein*: This is a collection from various statements on human spiritual nature from the Bahá'í Writings.

INDEX

A

'Abdu'l-Bahá, 17, 18, 22, 23, 25, 28, 29, 55, 76, 82, 127, 142, 145, 157, 166, 203, 219, 238, 241, 253, 255, 263, 265, 274
Abraham, 203
Adam, 8, 163, 174, 185, 235
Africa, 192
Akká, 26, 82
Alláh, 218
Anaximander, 42
Antimatter, 16
Aristotle, 63, 75, 78, 86, 117
Atheist, 189

B

Bahá'u'lláh, 18, 25, 26, 30, 86, 115, 145, 159, 191, 192, 203, 239, 241, 242, 248, 261, 274
Bahjí, 26
Berkeley, 96
Bethlehem, 196
Bible, 7, 8, *9*, 11, 13
Big Bang, *7, 8, 9, 10, 11, 12, 13, 15, 17, 21, 216*
Buddhism, 197, 211

C

Capitalist, 189
China, 96
Ching, 96
Christ, 192, 196, 197, 203
Christianity, 190, 196, 198, 211
Christians, 196
Creator, 15, 17, 55, 140, 169, 191, 215, 216, 217, 218, 221

D

Dark energy, 15, 16, 20, 21
Dark matter, 15, 16, 19, 21
Darwin, *41, 42, 43, 44, 46, 47, 48, 49*
Descartes, 75, 78, 90
DNA, 41, 43, 62, 65, 66, 67, 70, 87

E

Earth, 31, 41, 44, 49, 262
Education, 115, 169, 176, 177, 178, 179, 180, 182, 229
Ego, 105, 108
Egyptian, 192
Enlightenment, 75, 79, 96, 100
Europe, 192
Eve, 8
Evolution, 15, 17, 41, 44, 46

G

Galilee, 196
Genes, 66
Glial, 116
God, 2, 8, 23, 25, 28, 55, 86, 132, 187, 188, 190, 191, 192, 193, 194, 195, 196, 197, 200, 203, 206, 209, 215, 216, 217, 218, 219, 220, 221, 222,

223, 224, 225, 237, 238, 239, 240,
241, 242, 243, 245, 246, 248, 249,
255, 256, 263, 264, 268
Greece, 263
Greek philosophers, 42
Greeks, 192

H

Happiness, 251, 252, 253, 254
Harris, 189
Hinduism, 197, 198, 211
Homo sapiens, 44
Human reality, 53
Hume, 96

I

Identity, 7, 35, 84, 86, 87, 90, 93, 96, 97,
98, 100, 109, 266, 267
Imagination, 76, 80, 82, 83, 88, 89, 91,
92, 179, 231
India, 96, 192
Instinctive response, 64, 65, 67, 85, 101,
102, 129, 157, 160, 161, 178, 179,
263, 268
Intellectual reality, 2, 53, 55, 56, 61, 63,
73, 74, 75, 78, 80, 85, 98, 101, 115,
116, 118, 122, 168, 177, 179, 182,
194, 232
Írán, 26
Islám, 190, 218
Israel, 26, 192, 263, 268

J

James, 96
Jesus Christ, 197
John the Baptist, 196
Jordan River, 196
Judaism, 190, 197, 211, 218
Judea, 196
Junior youth, 261, 262, 265, 266, 267,
270, 271

K

Kant, 96, 100
Knowledge of God, 218, 219, 237, 240,
243, 245, 246, 248

L

Latin, 85, 90, 159, 177, 183, 188
Leibnitz, 96
Life, 23, 24, 25, 31, 32, 41, 44, 155, 243
Locke, 96
Love, 23, 25, 28, 34, 138, 139, 241, 242,
249
Love of God, 237, 238, 241

M

Manifestation of God, 26, 187, 188, 190,
192, 194, 196, 198, 219, 237, 238,
239, 240, 245, 246
Marx, 189
Matter, 15, 16, 19, 25
Messiah, 197
Moral choice, 91, 130
Moral feeling, 120, 122
Moses, 192, 203
Muḥammad, 192, 203
Mystical, 2, 213, 237

N

Nazareth, 196

P

Persian Empire, 263, 268
Physical reality, 53, 55, 56, 60, 74, 101,
118, 122, 182
Plato, 96, 100, 117
Prophet, 1, 18, 26, 86, 188, 191
Pythagora, 263

R

Religion, 187, 189, 192, 193, 199, 200,
210, 229, 237, 238
Revelation, 26, 203, 264
Romans, 192

S

Sacred Writing, 237, 238
Science, 27, 28, 54, 226, 228, 231
Self, 95, 96, 97

Self-respect, 141, 142
Sensory perception, 37, 62, 63, 68
Service, 146, 147, 243
Socrates, 117, 263, 268
Solomon, 192, 263
Spirit, 8, 23, 25, 28, 34, 37, 246
Spiritual cycle, 200
Spiritual development, 239
Spiritual perception, 87, 91
Spiritual reality, 53, 56, 61, 85, 101, 118, 122, 182, 231, 232, 233, 234
Spirituality, 226, 227, 228, 229, 231, 237
Summer, 201
Syrians, 192

T

The Báb, 203
The Bahá'í Faith, 198, 203, 211, 218, 219, 239, 243
The brain, 64
The mind, 1, 11, 23, 56, 63, 64, 73, 74, 75, 76, 78, 79, 80, 81, 82, 84, 85, 86, 87, 88, 90, 91, 93, 100, 101, 114, 116, 117, 118, 120, 126, 132, 141, 144, 145, 147, 148, 157, 160, 161, 168, 171, 172, 177, 179, 180, 183, 184, 189, 232, 240, 241, 255, 261, 262, 263, 267
Thought, 88

Transient happiness, 251, 253
True happiness, 251, 252, 254, 255

U

Understanding, 101, 138, 145
Universe, 7, 15, 20, 24, 55
Upanishads, 96

V

Virtues, 114, 117, 120, 121, 124, 138, 150, 238

W

Winter, 202

Y

Yahweh, 218

Z

Zoroastrianism, 197, 211

www.ingramcontent.com/pod-product-compliance
Lightning Source LLC
Chambersburg PA
CBHW060509300426
44112CB00017B/2600